THE ROUGH WITH THE SMOOTH

Nick Faldo
with Mitchell Platts

THE ROUGH
WITH THE SMOOTH

Breaking into Professional Golf

Foreword by Peter Oosterhuis

STANLEY PAUL
London Melbourne Sydney Auckland Johannesburg

Stanley Paul & Co. Ltd

An imprint of the Hutchinson Publishing Group

3 Fitzroy Square, London W1P 6JD

Hutchinson Group (Australia) Pty Ltd
30–32 Cremorne Street, Richmond South, Victoria 3121
PO Box 151, Broadway, New South Wales 2007

Hutchinson Group (NZ) Ltd
32–34 View Road, PO Box 40–086, Glenfield, Auckland 10

Hutchinson Group (SA) (Pty) Ltd
PO Box 337, Bergvlei 2012, South Africa

First published 1980
© Nick Faldo 1980

Set in Intertype Baskerville

Printed in Great Britain by The Anchor Press Ltd
and bound by Wm Brendon & Son Ltd,
both of Tiptree, Essex

ISBN 0 09 141760 0

Contents

	Acknowledgements	6
	Foreword by Peter Oosterhuis	7
1	Champion! – The Glorious Prize	9
2	Jack on the 'Box'	19
3	Outward Bound	24
4	Back to School	29
5	Space City	36
6	Cheers, Skol	41
7	The Big One	47
8	The Morning-After Feeling	57
9	Open '78	62
10	Ian Connelly	75
11	Aced by Jacko	80
12	The 'Walking One-Iron'	86
13	Seve and Me	94
14	The Wonders of Wentworth	102
15	Walton Heath Blues	110
16	Good Golly! Nick Faldo	119
17	Love and Augusta	126
18	Barry Willett – A Pro's Pro	135
19	Open '79	147
20	Ryder Cup Revival	155
21	Defying the Odds	168

Acknowledgements

I should particularly like to thank Mitchell Platts for all his help in the preparation of this book.

Thanks also to the following for permission to reproduce their excellent photographs: Peter Dazeley, who provided the bulk of them, F. Tewkesbury (*Evening Standard*), David Sandison and the *Daily Star*.

Foreword by Peter Oosterhuis

When I first met Nick Faldo at the Ryder Cup in 1977 I did not know what to expect. Through our long-time mutual friend Gerald Micklem I knew a little of Nick's great feats as an amateur and had followed his progress as a professional. It was immediately clear to me that, although this was his first Ryder Cup, always a nerve-racking experience, Nick was very sure of his ability and relished the challenge of the matches. Within hours of shaking hands for the first time Nick and I were practising together for that Ryder Cup at Royal Lytham and St Annes. I'm not sure why Brian Huggett, the team captain that year, paired us together. It just seemed to fall that way. In fact that Ryder Cup turned out to be a very rewarding experience for both of us. We were unbeaten in our three matches.

My experience probably helped Nick to settle down in our first match, the foursomes, in which we came from behind to beat Lou Graham and Ray Floyd. However the next day was a different story; as soon as we got into the fourball match, against Floyd and Jack Nicklaus, Nick oozed with confidence. We combined well through the round and won again. I loved every minute of that game, watching Nick play so many great shots and contributing a few myself. I remembered how excited I was to be playing well in my first Ryder Cup in 1971 at St Louis, and I could see Nick was now just as excited – it was great to be a part of that.

I don't think anyone was surprised when Nick easily won the Colgate PGA Championship in 1978 at Royal Birkdale. I was certainly not the only golf enthusiast who felt that this was just the beginning of great things for Nick Faldo. It seemed to be just another routine step up the ladder to the top of pro golf.

But golf can be the most humbling game. When Nick arrived at The Greenbrier in West Virginia for the 1979 Ryder Cup things had changed. His confidence had been threatened by an uninspiring year in Europe. To finish twenty-first in the Order of Merit was very poor by his standards. At The Greenbrier he showed that he could forget the past disappointments and, representing Britain and Europe, he came through superbly, winning three matches and losing one.

Nick had dominated the amateur scene in Britain during 1975 before taking the plunge into the professional game. I am sure it never occurred to him to enjoy another couple of years at the top of the amateur game.

Playing in the Home International matches, the Walker Cup and the Eisenhower Trophy is a great experience. But Nick decided to raise his sights and aim at the top of the professional game. That is the sort of man he is.

There will be other disappointments along the way to the top of professional golf for Nick, but he is very capable of taking the rough with the smooth.

I

Champion! – The Glorious Prize

Champion! The one word that means so much to a sports competitor. To Tom Watson in 1977 it became a byword. He won the US Masters at Augusta. He won four events on the demanding US tour. He topped the US money list with $310,653. And in Britain he won the Open – the world's oldest and most glittering golf title.

Champion! To me, Nick Faldo, it was a word buried with the treasured memories of my amateur days.

Yet Tom Watson and I were to meet that same year . . . and I was to win. And before that meeting I was to step on to the same tee as Jack Nicklaus – to most people the greatest player in the history of golf. Here was I, Nick Faldo, at 20 years of age in the company of Nicklaus, the player whose image on a television screen a few years earlier had fired me with the dream of becoming one of the world's top golfers.

My meetings with Watson and Nicklaus came in the 1977 Ryder Cup matches over one of my favourite courses – Royal Lytham and St Annes. It was my first appearance for the Great Britain and Ireland team against the United States in this historical match, and at the end of the contest I had maintained an unbeaten record. It confirmed for me that I could make it in the tough world of professional golf.

In 1977 there was not a better golfing scalp to be had than Watson's. A new era in the game had seemingly unfolded with Watson's win in the US Masters. He had squarely answered the pundits who had the audacity to question his ability under pressure. In the cauldron of Augusta, permanent home of the

Masters, and possibly the best course in America, he had finished 12 under par and 2 strokes ahead of the 'king' – Jack Nicklaus.

There was to follow a second encounter of the year between Nicklaus and the pretender to his throne: it came in the Open Championship at Turnberry in July. Nicklaus, keen to put Watson in his place, opened 68–70–65. But so had his rival. On the Saturday morning, all was quiet at Turnberry. Nicklaus and Watson teed off last, 3 shots ahead of Ben Crenshaw and 6 shots clear of the rest. It was simply a two-man battle for the title. And what a battle it turned out to be.

Watson, of course, won. But this incredible tussle was not decided until the very last hole. Watson had gone a stroke ahead, after Nicklaus had failed with a shortish putt on the 17th green. Watson, with the honour from the tee, was well placed on the fairway; Nicklaus, risking everything with his driver, had seen the ball trickle under gorse bushes on the right. It seemed all over. But Nicklaus kept the crowd in suspense by hitting an incredible shot to the green. It still seemed hopeless, for Watson's second, a seven-iron from 178 yards, finished within 2 feet of the hole. Then, from more than 30 feet, Nicklaus holed an amazing putt for a birdie 3, and even Watson must have been shaken. But, cool and clear-headed, Watson holed the putt for victory.

Champion! The word echoed in Watson's ears. The crowd cheered and whistled. Millions, watching the drama on television, slumped back in their armchairs exhausted. Watson grinned. Nicklaus, gracious in defeat, warmly congratulated his rival. Watson, the crowd still roaring, collected the magnificent trophy. I just drove south and home.

I wasn't jealous. I was disappointed. Twelve months earlier I had appeared in my first Open. It was a marvellous occasion and the biggest moment, at that time, in my golfing career. And I had crowned it with a final round of 69 to finish joint twenty-eighth with Gary Player, Doug Sanders and Neil Coles. Naturally, I could look back and analyse how I could have done better. I did nothing spectacular at Royal Birkdale, but for the first time it wasn't a bad performance. If I had been 2 strokes better I would have won nearly £1000 instead of £335.

So I was deflated as I left Turnberry after shooting rounds of 71, 76, 74 and 78 to finish joint sixty-second. It was a backward step – and I didn't enjoy it. In a way it was my own fault because I had arrived at this beautiful course a little bit carried away. I had come almost straight from losing a play-off to Seve Ballesteros for the Uniroyal International title at Moor Park and I reckoned if I kept my form I would win. Of course, golf is not like that. Turnberry was a far different test from Moor Park. This Ayrshire course venue was a tough links compared with the comparative gentleness of the Hertfordshire circuit.

It was the Uniroyal tournament in June which virtually secured my place in the 1977 Ryder Cup and my eventual clash with Watson. My friend and teacher Ian Connelly had said to me at the start of the year, 'Let's make that Ryder Cup team.' It looked the correct target at which to aim, but really it seemed only a dream. But by the time I got to the Uniroyal it was beginning to look a possibility. I had finished joint third in the Madrid Open in April and joint sixth in the Colgate PGA Championship at Royal St George's, Sandwich, in May. And in between I had reached the fifth round of the Sun Alliance Match Play Championship at Stoke Poges, near Slough, before being beaten by Brian Huggett. Ironically Brian was to be my captain in the Ryder Cup.

So I had won around £4000, which had put me in the running – the Ryder Cup merit table is based on 1 point for every £1 won. It was now a case of plodding on, but there was certainly nothing pedestrian about the Uniroyal. In fact, I reckoned at the time that I was on a victory march and it certainly looked that way to most people for much of the time. From the start of the week, I was bubbling inside. I had a feeling that this was going to be the big breakthrough. I knew Moor Park well, because it was no more than a half-hour's drive away from home and I had played in several Hertfordshire Colts matches there during my amateur days. And my game was good.

I opened with rounds of 68 and 67. After the second day, when I had eight birdies and everything went right, I found myself 4 shots clear of Greg Norman of Australia. I must admit I suddenly began to wonder what was happening to me. I knew I was in the lead and I suppose I felt a little edgy. My swing got a little too quick during the third round and my caddie had to keep reminding me to slow down. But in that kind of situation it is easier said than done. I needed to make an effort. Suddenly the swing was no longer automatic. I finished with 73 – not too bad, I suppose – but Seve Ballesteros, after opening with a couple of 70s, reeled off a 67 to take a 1 stroke lead.

When the last day dawned I still felt confident. It did not bother me that the golf world were wondering if I could win. I knew that what I needed to discover was how I would react under intense pressure. I had never experienced anything like this before. I'm sure that day helped my career. When I met Watson three months later I found out that I could stick at it under pressure. I didn't choke against Seve. I was never scared. But I did lose.

Looking back, I reckon the biggest drawback I faced that day was not partnering Seve. I had a great player as my partner in Australian Graham Marsh, but since Seve was in the lead – and that was where I had hoped to be – I'm sure it would have been better to play with him. I made a great start and after 4 holes I was in a 3 shot lead . . . but I didn't know it. There were no leader boards on the front 9 holes and I didn't realize Seve had dropped back. It was only on the back 9 that I began to get 'reports' on Seve. The news filtered through, as it always does on the caddie grapevine, that Seve was hitting the ball all over the place but still getting the right figures. It was typical stuff and I arrived at the 18th tee to see the leader board reading . . . – 12 BALLESTEROS – 11 FALDO.

The 18th at Moor Park is a short, downhill par 3 hole which requires a positive tee shot. I had to make a 2, but my tee shot finished 18 feet or so from the stick and it left me with the kind of putt you can do without. It looked impossible. It was fast. It had a 2 foot break. And, if I missed, the ball would go 5 or 6 feet past. So I might finish with a 4 and that would give Seve, playing behind me a cushion, and the title would surely be his. There was nothing to do but to be bold. And fortunately the only thing I was thinking about was holing the putt. I don't think I heard the cheers that went up as the ball dropped, but I knew for certain the ball was in the hole. And that was all that mattered.

Thirty minutes later it was a different Nick Faldo. I had been beaten in the play-off by Seve. Beaten when victory had seemed certain to be mine. The 508 yard 16th was chosen as the first extra hole and Seve knocked his drive left off the tee into rough. I hit a solid tee shot and then drilled a three-wood under branches and the ball rolled up to just off the back of the green. Seve? His second was now hooking. It looked all over – but the ball struck a spectator and he was left a pitch to the green. Seve doesn't make many errors with those shots and he wedged up to 4 feet. I still held the advantage because I had a putt for the title. To this day I don't know what happened with it. The ball seemed to race off the putter. Over the first couple of feet it gathered momentum so quickly that although it was on the right line it finished 12 feet past the hole. The return stayed on the lip; Seve holed and the title was his.

It was bitterly disappointing. I reckon that if I had won the Uniroyal my career might have taken off quicker. It would have been great to get that big 72 hole win under my belt so early. The only consolation was that, whereas I had been a 'nobody' on the tour in the eyes of the public, I had now made my mark. And the £3750 cheque made me almost certain to qualify for the Ryder Cup team.

With two events remaining in the Ryder Cup points race, I thought I might be challenged by either Sam Torrance or Doug McClelland. At the time I had no intention of playing in the Dutch Open in August – the last points counting tournament – and so I knew I had to secure the situation for myself the previous week in the German Open at Düsseldorf. Tony Gray, one of the tournament directors, said there was still time if I wanted to enter for the Dutch Open. But in the end I just shut my mind to everything else but the tournament on hand in Düsseldorf, shot two closing rounds of 68 and finished joint third to win my Ryder Cup place and not have to bother competing in Holland. I was pleased as punch.

Exactly one month later and one week before the Ryder Cup on 15 September I had glandular fever. I didn't know it at the time. I had gone to play in the Tournament Players' Championship over the Foxhills course near Chertsey in Surrey and

I found myself totally listless. I knew I was tired but I had never felt this exhausted. My mother had driven me down the previous Monday from a tournament at the Hill Valley course in Shropshire because I had a terrible pain in my neck and she had taken me to see a doctor. He told me to take a break. But I said that I had to play in the TPC to keep my game sharp for the Ryder Cup. So he told me not to practise but to sit in a chair and rest before going out. Then he phoned my mother later at home and told her I had glandular fever.

But nobody told me. I suppose they thought it might frighten me. But I knew that something was wrong. The first day at Foxhills was horrible. It was very strange because I would go bogey-bogey-double bogey-bogey without a care in the world. Then, for some reason, I would suddenly feel fit as a fiddle and wonder what the hell I was doing. But I finished with an 80. I was very depressed, not only with my own game but also because my partner was Brian Huggett – my captain at Royal Lytham the following week.

That night I wondered what he would think of me. He had already made it crystal clear, through the press, that he was quite prepared to ignore the younger members in the squad if they did not appear to be in form or up to the pressure of competing against the Americans. However, the next day I did myself a bit of good by shooting 71. But twenty-four hours later I was out of the event. I retired after taking 82 in the third round when things went from bad to worse to terrible. I felt dreadful. And I was due to report in two days to the Ryder Cup camp.

When I got to the hotel at Royal Lytham and St Annes I was not feeling too bad. Two days' rest had done me the world of good and I didn't think any more of the so-called illness. I still had no idea what it was – only that it made me feel extremely weary. The only thing on my mind now was the Ryder Cup. It was my first time and I was really looking forward to the challenge of the next few days. It was not only the thought of playing against the superstars from the United States that appealed to me; it was also the challenge of actually proving to skipper 'Huggy' that I was strong and ready to handle the special pressures associated with this particular match. I wanted to show him that I could win for my country, that I could help us become the first Great Britain and Ireland team to win the Ryder Cup since the 1957 team captained by Dai Rees won at Lindrick. It was going to be a special week.

Then, on the Wednesday, the day before the match began, I woke up with a rash on all my pressure points. At first I just saw these smudge-like marks on my fingers. Then I noticed my wrists had the same kind of rash. And my knees and elbows. I didn't know what to do. I wondered whether it was nerves. I wondered whether it was a recurrence of the illness. I could not believe that it had happened to me. This was the biggest week of my life. The week in which I would represent my country in the Ryder Cup. It was like being the star of a new show in the West End and finding out that your understudy might be needed for the first night. And there was no way I wanted that curtain to go up without me.

I decided I would not tell a soul. I reckoned I could cover up the rash and make out that nothing was wrong. I looked in the bathroom mirror. No, I didn't look ill in the face. And I certainly didn't feel ill. So I felt certain that I could get away with it. Then I suddenly wondered – what if there is something serious wrong with me? What if I fall really ill on the golf course and collapse? Wouldn't it be embarrassing to be rushed to hospital in an ambulance! So I decided I had better find out. I sat in a chair trying to convince myself that I had to tell somebody. I grabbed a club and found I couldn't hold it. The rash was all over my fingers. I couldn't hide that – and I certainly couldn't play anyway. So I picked up the phone and I asked reception for Brian Huggett's room.

'Huggy,' I said. 'It's Nick. I'm covered in a rash.' There was a moment's silence, then –

'Hell! I'd better get the doctor along to see you. He's coming to see Jacko [Tony Jacklin] because he's got a cold. So I'll send him up to you afterwards.'

The doc eventually arrived. He took a look at me and did a blood test. Then he pronounced, 'Lad, you've got glandular fever.'

Well, I got straight on the phone to my mother. I said, 'Mum, I've got glandular fever,' and she said, 'Yes, I know, son.'

In fact Mum and Dad had kept the whole thing a complete

secret. Our doctor had told them that there was no point worrying me with it. It seems there is no instant cure. You just have to rest and build yourself up.

I didn't have time for that at Royal Lytham. But I spent the next couple of hours in the room and the rash began to disappear. Then the thought of the match began to dawn on me and I forgot about glandular fever. I went out for the final practice session and Huggett came up to me on the 14th fairway and said, 'You and Peter [Oosterhuis] are playing together tomorrow. Good luck.'

It was great to find out that I was going to start the Ryder Cup in action in the foursomes. But it was strange how captain Huggett kept the team selection a closely guarded secret, even amongst the team, until the last afternoon. He played a bit of a cat-and-mouse game and nobody seemed to know what was happening. We all wanted to know as early as possible what the pairings were going to be. It is much better that way, so that you can adjust yourself either to playing or sitting it out. Now Oosty and I had to work out our game plan for the first day foursomes match against Ray Floyd and Lou Graham.

For Oosty, former British number one, it was a little like meeting a couple of old pals, for he was now a regular on the US tour. But for me it hit hard that I was playing a man who had won the US Open in 1975 (Graham) and another who had won the US Masters in 1976 (Floyd). And, on top of that, it was decided that since I was driving the ball better than Oosty I should tee off at the 1st. It was a real nerve-racker. That morning in practice I hit twenty extra four-irons and twenty extra five-irons to make sure that I was ready for that first hole. It is not a particularly difficult hole – a par 3 of 206 yards. But the railway on the right is out of bounds and the green is protected by bunkers. And I didn't want to make a mess of it. In the end I did just that – but not with the tee shot!

I struck the ball well, but it went a little to the left and Oosty left me with a 3 foot putt to hole and halve the 1st. I missed. All I could hear were the groans of the crowd. The 'here-we-go-again' chorus rattled in my ears. But I was unperturbed. I knew I had struck a solid putt but it was just one of those occasions when, as luck would have it, the ball stayed out. And

Ian Connelly, squatting at the edge of the green, gave me a wink and mouthed, 'Don't worry.'

I didn't and at the end of the day we were the only home winners. We had beaten Floyd and Graham 2 and 1. I was overjoyed.

That ensured that I played on the second day. And this time Oosty and I drew the big one – Floyd and Nicklaus in the fourballs. I couldn't believe it. Everything was suddenly happening for Nick Faldo. And I still have to laugh about that match. At Oosty's own admission he just left it to me for the first 7 holes. I put us in the lead at the 2nd, hitting the green with one of my best two-iron shots, and then kept up a steady game, which included out-driving the mighty Floyd and Nicklaus. I was really enjoying myself, but it was nice to welcome Oosty back into the game at the 8th and 9th where he came alive and we took command. We never looked back. And at the end of the day we were again the only winners in the Great Britain and Ireland camp – triumphing 3 and 1. The team, however, was trailing by 5 points overall and the writing was on the wall. The twelve singles seemed unlikely to change the destiny of Sam Ryder's Cup for another year – but I found myself in the situation of being able to rubber-stamp an amazing Ryder Cup début. I had drawn Watson in the singles.

I stress the point *drawn* because that is exactly the way it happened – unless somebody has kept something from me. There was a feeling that it had been fixed. I was questioned on whether or not the draw had been made to give television a boost on the final day. That theory, I suppose, was partly expressed because Huggett chose to put Oosty and me out ninth and tenth. There was a school of thought that since – at least taking the results of the first two days as a guide – we were the men in form we should be at the head of the field. What was the point in putting us out last when the match might be decided early on? By this time the Americans needed only to take three of the ten singles to win the match. It was Huggett's belief that Oosty and I would be better employed as 'tail-enders' because in that position we could bring the team through if there was a chance of victory. It was a theory that was not popular with a lot of people – including the British press. And on top of that, Huggett also left out Tony Jacklin.

But, much as I would have loved Great Britain and Ireland to have won, I have to admit that I closed my mind a little on that possibility in order to concentrate entirely on overcoming Watson. This was my big chance to make an impact. I had won two matches in the Ryder Cup, but both of them had been in the company of Peter Oosterhuis. And there could be little doubt that his experience helped me. Now I was on my own against 1977's number one golfer of the year. This was a dream come true. Tom Watson was a household name – on both sides of the Atlantic. I was just a lad playing the Open Champion. I went to the first tee telling myself I had to win.

My mood never changed. I won the 4th with a par 4 and I went 2 up with an eagle 3 at the 486 yard 6th. True, I lost the 7th and 9th but I never lost my confidence. I felt that I was in the driving seat and that there was no way I was going to allow him to take control. I got the initiative back with a birdie 3 at the 334 yard 10th and a real boost with a 2 at the 201 yard 12th which is reckoned by a lot of the top players to be one of the hardest par 3s in the country. It is certainly the toughest at Royal Lytham. Now I was 2 up, the United States had won the match but a famous victory was mine if I remained calm.

Watson, however, was not ready to succumb. He won the 14th and he took the demanding 17th, the hole with a plaque in a bunker marking the spot from which the legendary Bobby Jones struck a wonder-shot to turn the destiny of the 1926 Open in his favour. Now it all rested on the 18th. I had no worries. I felt certain that I could make a par 4; and I had a sneaking feeling that I was going to make 3. In the end a 4 was good enough because Watson bunkered his final drive and victory was mine. It was a fabulous feeling and I walked off that final green with the cheers of the crowd ringing in my ears just as they had for Watson up the coastline in the Open a couple of months earlier.

I had beaten the 1977 US Masters and Open Champion and had won all my matches. The door had finally swung wide enough to allow me a glimpse of the future. I liked what I saw . . . but I soon found out that it was not to be that easy.

2
Jack on the 'Box'

I suppose there is a time in most people's lives to which they look back and pinpoint the moment when their future was decided. Well the point of time when my 'Jack-in-the-Box' emerged to point me in the right direction was ironically when Jack was actually on the 'Box'.

It was Easter, 1971, and I was almost 14 years old. Usually I wouldn't give the television a second look because I was a sports fanatic and I always seemed to be swimming, cycling, running or playing football, cricket or basketball. So I didn't give myself much time to sit down in front of the telly. But my parents had gone in for a colour television and, as anything new always does in the family home, it was momentarily commanding our everyday interest.

I'll never forget the picture I saw. It was of Jack Nicklaus striking a ball with a background of lovely green trees. It was Augusta – the home of the US Masters. It was golf – the game which was to transform my life.

In fact my life had begun at 285 Knella Road, Welwyn Garden City, in Hertfordshire. I was born there on 18 July 1957. My parents lived in a council house but my father reckoned that somewhere in Britain there had to be a mansion which belonged to us! He had traced back the family tree and he discovered that the Faldos had come over from Italy during the 17th century. But he went back farther than that and he found out that four centuries earlier there was a certain Sir William Faldo. It would appear that he was a knight of some rank and so my dad always maintains that 'some fool must have lost all our money somewhere'. Still my father, George, who worked as a financial planner for ICI in Welwyn Garden

City, and my mother, Joyce, were both quite happy in Knella Road. And I hope even happier when I came along!

No. 285 Knella Road was an end-of-terrace house. My parents had moved in a couple of years after getting married. There were two bedrooms, both rather cramped, but the kitchen was spacious and we also had the privilege of possessing an outhouse. The garden was also the biggest among this particular stretch of housing and I can remember that my friends often came over to play because we had the space to build camps and enjoy ourselves. But I'll never forget that my mum had one strict rule. We were not allowed to scream! It was not a case of noise; it was a mother's protective instinct. She reckoned that if someone screamed they must be hurt. So she only wanted to hear screaming if it was the real thing. Then she came running!

I suppose, like all mums, she was relatively happy to get me off her hands when, at the age of 3, I went to nursery school. My real schooling days began when I went to Thumbswood, the local primary school, at the age of 5. I stayed there only two years before moving on to Blackthorn, which was a well-disciplined school but I enjoyed life there. I was also fortunate in that a new estate sprang up across the road from where we lived and there were plenty of boys – and girls – of my own age. My best friend at that time was Dereck Snellgrove. I shall never forget him because, at the age of 7, his life was transformed when he underwent a successful hole-in-the-heart operation.

At Blackthorn my sporting life centred on throwing a cricket ball! I was pretty big in those days – certainly for my age – and I could heave the ball a good bit farther than anybody else at the school. But I used to get rather complacent, and one day when I wandered off, as I had become bored waiting to compete in a qualifying competition for the Mid-Herts cricket-ball-throwing contest, a teacher came looking for me, grabbed me by the ear and took me in his car back to the field where the competition was taking place. I've since learned, of course, that you should never be complacent. Nevertheless I still won that particular event . . . with one throw!

Winning a cricket-ball contest meant a lot to me, even at that age. I hated to lose at anything. There was nothing that made me feel worse. And I would do anything to ensure that

I had the best possible chance of being on the winning side. I once belonged to a team at school which got hammered. So the next year I was desperate not to appear for that particular team again and insisted I belonged to another team. Well, I got my wish . . . and the team I'd left walked away with the prizes! It was about what I deserved.

I was enjoying my school life at that time. When I was 5 or 6 I had been a bit of a tearaway, but I had mellowed a little. I firmly believe that it was sport that made me buckle down, because at the age of 6 I started swimming and you couldn't keep me out of the water. Then, at the age of 10, I began to experience that wonderful glow that floods through your body when you know you are the best. First, I became the only boy in the history of the school to get a gold medal for life-saving. Secondly, after weeks of training in a small pool at Hatfield, I won the Herts County Boys 110 yards free-style. I was elated – and not just because my appearances in the pool were restricting my classroom attendance! I had found something I could dominate. And it was a great feeling.

My world came crashing down a few weeks later at Crystal Palace. My win in the Herts County Championship meant that I would represent the county in the national finals. When I arrived at Crystal Palace I could not believe my eyes. It was like an ocean compared with Welwyn Garden City swimming pool where I trained. When I stood on the edge of the pool waiting to dive in I could feel the nerves tightening my stomach muscles. At that time I didn't realize that this was to be my first big test as I worked towards a career in sport, that there would be many more occasions when I would have to grit my teeth and grind out my performance in a sporting arena. The next moment – splash, and I was in the water swimming as hard and as fast as I could. I think I swam faster than ever before but I still finished fourth. I had lost. I was deflated. But my instructors at Welwyn Garden City, Mrs Last and Reg Potter, an Olympic water-polo player, quickly pointed out that it was a good performance. And I went home happy.

It was now time for me to change schools again and, in spite of missing quite a few lessons because of my sporting timetable, I passed my exams and went to Sir Frederic Osborn Comprehensive School. The day before I was due to put on my new uniform for the first time we moved house. My father had scrimped and saved every penny to raise the necessary deposit to buy No. 11 Redwoods in Welwyn Garden City for £5200. It was a big move, at the time, for my parents and, looking back, it was important because it pushed us farther out into the country where, in a few years' time, it was possible for me to devote all my energy to one activity – golf.

We were now living in a completely different area. Our house had three bedrooms and it was in the middle of a nice terrace at the bottom of a close. We had a smart garden with fancy-shaped cut grass and a patio walled off with fir trees. Across the road, in Stonemead, were the big houses – six-bedroom affairs. I'm told that three of the twelve houses in that particular road were occupied by millionaires. What is for certain is that my ambitious nature began to be stimulated at this time. One day, I told myself, I would live in a big house.

I thoroughly enjoyed my upbringing. The family holidays had to be run on a tight budget, but my dad purchased an Austin A40 and we went off on camping holidays to France, touring the Loire area, and to Sheringham in Norfolk. Most importantly, my parents encouraged me to take part in sport. My first games teacher, a Mr Harvey, had written on my first school report: 'Nick's future will be in sport. He sets his standards high and his dedication will be the key to his success.' They were words my parents seemed to heed.

I played basketball, soccer and cricket. At soccer I started at left-back, but later went into goal. I suppose I reckoned that at the last line of defence I would have the final say in the match. It was my way of showing that I was an individual. I played cricket, not exactly brilliantly, but not too badly. I was also a bit of an athlete, running at 800 metres and 1500 metres, and my best time for the mile was 5 minutes 16 seconds. I threw the discus and javelin and, on occasions, took part in the shot putt.

I also loved cycling; I worked hard at that sport out of school time and I managed to graduate to grade four, which is considered to be one step away from the standard at which the instructors sit up and take notice. If I had worked even harder it is possible that I might have made it to international standard. But that is something I shall never know. In truth, I was a sports enthusiast, but my only contact with golf had been at the age of 8 when my grandfather gave me a hickory two-iron which I used to make clearings for camps in the woods! I wish I still had it because it would be a prize possession in my golf equipment room at home. It would have come in pretty useful the day after I saw Jack Nicklaus on television. Because from that moment I was bitten by the golf bug. And I was already dreaming of becoming a golfing superstar.

3
Outward Bound

Growing up is hard to define. Is it something that happens automatically? Or is it a case of a point in your life giving you a *raison d'être*? My mother believes I grew up when I was chosen to go on a Duke of Edinburgh Outward Bound course. She maintains; 'Nick went away as a boy and he came back a man.'

I went off for a month at Ullswater in the Lake District, in the Easter of 1972. The first night was freezing and all the boys on the course went to sleep with teeth chattering. Then, after being in bed for less than an hour, a bell rang out and somebody cried, 'Fire!'

We ran out of our wooden hut to discover it was just an exercise. If that was not a painful enough introduction to our month away, we were ordered out of our beds at 6 a.m. and marched straight into a cold shower. We were told afterwards that we had to be ready for all emergencies – and that would include capsizing from a dinghy into the ice-cold waters of a lake.

The first two weeks actually turned out marvellously, with the weather boiling hot. Then the weather broke and it snowed. Two feet of snow piled up in no time at all. Suddenly it was no longer a picnic. We were about to take our three-day 'unescorted' survival test – and freezing rain followed to make things even tougher. This was the real eye-opener – the spell which really transformed me. I had been playing golf for a year – hooked on the game itself. But there was still something missing. I believe that one month in the Lake District changed me from being an average lad in the street to one desperately wanting an aim in life. It gave me ambition. It made me realize that you can't take the easy path all that time. I began to understand that only hard work and dedication would ensure that, in time, I was a master of my chosen craft. And that was golf.

I have always been a bit of a loner and golf now seemed to be a natural choice. As a kid I had begun to hate playing soccer because I got so furious when we lost. I felt really down when I trudged off the field a loser. My parents knew how I felt because when I arrived back after a match I used to sit down and get more and more depressed. So when I told them I wanted to be a golfer I think they were truly thankful that I had something else to occupy my mind. My father was busy at work and so it was my mother who made the early moves. Neither of us really knew how I should go about becoming a golfer and so my mother said that the only way to find out was to go up to the local club at Welwyn Garden City and simply ask. She also stressed that in return for taking me along I must have my hair cut!

So one morning we went to the hairdresser's and in the afternoon we met Chris Arnold, the assistant professional at Welwyn Garden City Golf Club. He told us that it was best to have half a dozen lessons – good advice – before buying any equipment. That way a beginner could determine whether or not he wanted to continue and it was only going to cost the price of the instruction. Me? I was raring to go. I wanted my first lesson that afternoon, but Chris was fully booked and he said to come back tomorrow.

I couldn't wait to get back to the club. And I took to golf like a duck takes to water. But I think I have a lot to thank Chris for, because he went about it in just the right way. For the first four or five lessons he would not let me hit a ball. Not one ball. Instead we just stood on the practice ground and he taught me the rudiments of the game, such as grip and stance. I was allowed to swing a club but I was not allowed to hit a ball. It was a great idea because it taught one that the ball is not a target. It is something that just sits there in front of you for you to swing at and swish away.

If my memory serves me well it was on the fifth lesson that I was finally allowed to strike a ball. And I think I rather stunned Chris because I didn't have a single air-shot. In fact, he should have been proud. Because it was his insistence that I didn't hit a single ball until I could control the club which ultimately led to my striking those first few shots with a certain authority. I began to imagine myself as Jack Nicklaus hitting to the 18th green and winning the US Masters.

Chris and I became very friendly. But lessons at that time cost about 50p a time and for my parents it was becoming a costly affair. I can remember standing on the practice ground and hitting golf shots until my hands were cut, sore and bleeding. So that meant money for a glove. Then, on another occasion, I returned home with my ordinary walking shoes soaked through. So my parents had to pay for a pair of golf shoes.

We were lucky in that a neighbour at that time was Graham Thomas, who had been my deputy headmaster at Blackthorn Primary School and was also interested in golf. He played a little and when he learned that I was interested he went hunting in his garage and came back with ladies' seven- and eight-irons. They were my first clubs and I was delighted. I would carry them with me everywhere, together with a bag of balls which I had gathered from rummaging through the bushes on the course. My mother, who worked at a school in Ware, also told one of the lady teachers that I had taken up golf and she sent over a selection of golf balls. It was nice of her – but they were absolutely cut to ribbons!

But they were better than nothing and in my bag, made by my mother out of a piece of old material, I would carry them across the road to the playing field where I would practise. The playing field belonged to Monkswalk School, but I obtained permission from the headmaster and I used to try to strike the balls down the line of the football pitch. Just beyond the pitch there was a long-jump pit and I practised trying to land all the balls in the sand. I suppose it was about 100 yards away from where I was hitting them and my record was 15 out of 18. I can remember that because I used to get annoyed that I couldn't do better.

It wasn't long before I put my name forward for membership of Welwyn Garden City Golf Club. Then on my 14th birthday I received from my parents a half-set of 'St Andrews' junior clubs. My parents had 'sneaked' up to Welwyn to see the professional, Ian Connelly, to ask him whether or not it was wise to invest in a set of clubs. Ian apparently told them that I seemed to like the game and so Father wrote out a cheque for £35 and I was away. I think Ian also gave them a little blue carrying-bag which had belonged to his father.

When I was given the clubs I could hardly wait to get out of the house. I raced up to the course to have my first round on my own. I was a little worried at the close proximity of the clubhouse and the fact that I might make a mess of things with somebody watching. But I was more worried when I reached the 1st green. The sprinklers were on and water was spraying everywhere. I thought, 'Hell, I shouldn't be here.' So I nipped round to the 2nd tee and missed putting out. But it was the same at the 2nd green, and I didn't tread on a real green until I reached the 3rd. It was a funny sensation. The grass was so soft and I felt as if I should be wearing carpet slippers and not spiked shoes.

How did I fare that first time? Well, I hit the ball seventy-eight times but I lost three balls and I didn't count all the putts. So I decided that as I would never do it that way again I wouldn't count it!

My game progressed through playing in the junior competition at Welwyn Garden City. Ironically, the captain of the juniors was John Moorhouse, who later became my caddie on the tour until we decided to part company in the winter of 1979–80. I used to play with John and his brother Colin and Trevor Powell, who now plays the tour himself. It was good experience for me because all three had been playing the game for around three years.

There is a school of thought that the Spaniards, like Severiano Ballesteros, Manuel Pinero and Antonio Garrido, have made it to the top because of their dedication as youngsters. It is said that they would practise the tough shots rather than just stand on the practice tee hitting balls. In other words they would bet each other pesetas that they couldn't get the ball into the cup from the most unfavourable lies. I don't doubt that for a minute. It will have certainly sharpened their short games. But back in the early seventies we were also doing it.

John, Colin, Trevor and I would stand in bunkers for hours

trying to play specific shots. And we would throw balls into bushes and see who could play the best recovery shots. Unfortunately the members at Welwyn Garden City took a poor view of this. It was 'just not golf' having juniors hitting balls out of bushes and making a mess of the practice sand trap! When we played as a fourball we were often told we were holding up senior members. Nothing was farther from the truth.

On one occasion when I was 15 I actually got banned from club competitions for one month when I was playing in a club medal with a senior member. We were due to tee off at the 10th and on reaching the tee I popped my head through the bushes to see if anybody was coming up the 9th and close enough to be called through. There was a party coming up, which included a committe member, but since they were a fourball and we were only a threeball it seemed reasonable that we should get going.

By this time I was playing off 5 and I finished with a net 67 and it was good enough to win the medal. But when I walked in I was told, 'Sorry, you're disqualified.' I was told I had played from the wrong tee. I never played another medal at Welwyn Garden City. I had the feeling that the committee had little time for the junior members of the club. But when Clive Harkett came along he gave the junior section tremendous support and he proved that juniors and seniors could live together.

Clive Harkett also inspired confidence in me and together with the support of my parents and the coaching of Ian Connelly I was moving towards 1975 – the year in which my career was to take off. Before that, I had been gaining a name for myself in Hertfordshire junior golf, playing for the Colts and competing competently, if not with any outstanding success, in junior Open meetings at a number of clubs. All the time, my handicap was coming down, from 5 to 4 to 3, and I felt really proud when I was selected as an England boy international in 1974. I was also chosen for the Hertfordshire senior county team, playing against some of the best amateur players from other counties, and my game was really becoming solid and satisfying.

4
Back to School

On 1 April 1975, I was a comparative golfing unknown. Eight months later Clive Harkett, captain of Welwyn Garden City Golf Club, was toasting the Queen at a celebration dinner for Nick Faldo. The dinner took place on 21 December and marked my major achievements in 1975. I still had to pinch myself to make sure that the last eight months were reality and not a dream.

I had won the English Amateur Championship, the South African Amateur Stroke Play Championship, the British Youths Championship, the Berkshire Trophy, the Scrutton Jug, the Champion of Champions Trophy, the Hertfordshire County Championship, the Hertfordshire Boys Championship, the Royston Junior Championship, the Welwyn Garden City GC Championship and I had tied for first place in the King George V Coronation Cup. I had also been selected and played for both England and British Youths sides, for England in the Home International series and for the British Commonwealth Trophy side in South Africa.

There is one big amateur week missing from the list. It is the Walker Cup. But when the match between Great Britain and Ireland against the United States was played in May of that year my name was known to few of the selectors and so I was not even considered for the side. But six days after the Walker Cup, I made headlines in the *Daily Express*. FALDO THE GREAT SHATTERS CUP ACE was the headline. Nick Faldo, a golfing unknown, had knocked John Davies, one of Britain's top players and a Walker Cup man, out of the Amateur Championship in the third round at Hoylake.

I was watched that day by Michael Bonallack, the new Walker Cup chief selector. But he was not to have the opportunity of picking me for a Walker Cup team because by the time the next match came round in 1977 I had turned professional. Nevertheless, that win over John Davies was a landmark. It meant more to me than just making the national newspapers. It meant more to me than simply proving to the outside world what I knew myself – that I could make it to the top. What it did was to sharpen my desire to aim for nothing less than the number one spot. I honestly believe that unless you make such a commitment to yourself in your chosen profession it is impossible to become the best.

My ego was also given a considerable boost. I had left John Davies gaping in disbelief with my 5 and 4 win, but like a true sportsman he recovered his composure and gave the waiting golf correspondents an astonishing assessment of his opponent. John said, 'I have just been beaten by the best amateur I have ever seen. What a boy! What class! He is better than all these Americans and he is good enough to win this week. He has a great temperament. If I can find a chink in the armour of anyone I play, I'll always attack it. But there was nothing I could do about him – he had no weaknesses.'

I especially liked those last few words. John had won the 1st hole, but I had countered with six birdies on the way to reaching the turn and forging 3 up. It was then that he began to try to employ his experience. He had Willie Aitchieson, one of golf's top caddies, with him, and together they began to chat a lot with me. Then they would walk ever so slowly down the fairway. They were using what we call match-play tactics. It had never happened to me before.

Playing for the Herts Colts did not have the same competitive edge. But I did recall being told by my Hertfordshire county captain of one remarkable match in which one player made a habit of taking his time on the greens. It was a method he used to disturb the concentration of his opponents. But on this occasion his rival went prepared to strike back. When the player began to pace around the green with the speed of a tortoise, his opponent walked across to his bag, unzipped a pocket and took out a shooting stick and a book. Then he perched himself on the side of the green and began to read.

The other man was so demoralized by the incident that he completely lost his own game and he was well beaten.

It was a story which played an important part in my game that afternoon. I suspected that John was trying to destroy my rhythm and he admitted afterwards that he was looking for a chink in my armour. It is not unfair and on another person it might have worked that day. But I refused to be shunted out of my groove and it was not long before I snatched another birdie and I ended the match. I was soon brought down to earth twenty-four hours later when I lost to David Moffatt at the 19th hole in the fourth round.

I was more than a little disappointed at losing. But I realized that it was only part of learning my trade and I was prepared to accept that it was another lesson in the hard grind to the top. I'm sure that it proved to be a valuable one because only a few weeks later I enjoyed my most rewarding success of that memorable year. I won the English Amateur Championship.

It was a thrilling turnabout in fortune for me, as I had arrived at Royal Lytham after failing to qualify for a place in the Open Championship at Carnoustie by the slender margin of 2 strokes. I had wanted so much to be a part of the Open, but it was not to be. But I did ensure that my trip to Scotland was not wasted. From Monifieth, where I had attempted to qualify with my friend Peter Little, I raced over to Carnoustie to watch the superstars in practice.

Jack Nicklaus and Tom Weiskopf were the first players I saw and later the same day I came across Tom Watson. He was a good player then, but he was not being assessed that year as the man who would challenge Nicklaus for the world number one spot. In fact he was a 33–1 bet to win the Open. But I was immediately impressed by the power of his arms and legs. It brought it home to me that I had to concentrate on building up strength in these areas. Of course, Watson made his big breakthrough that week when he beat Australian Jack Newton in a play-off for the title on the Sunday after the pair had tied for first place the previous day.

I was also fortunate enough to be introduced to Lee Trevino. Willie Aitchieson was caddying for Lee that week and he gave me the intro. It led to a marvellous afternoon. I walked the course with Lee and was treated not only to a close-up look at his game but he also gave me his whole life story. With Lee it is laughs all the way but I was able to listen and learn from the man who had twice won the Open, in 1971 and 1972.

That week I could not believe my luck. I was watching Johnny Miller during one of his practice rounds and he came over to talk to me. Johnny was the new golden boy of golf. The previous year he had won a record $353,021 on the United States tour – I had been laying carpets with my mate Ron Marks and earning a few quid! Yet now the two of us were walking the fairways of Carnoustie together. I wasn't playing, but it gave me a chance to have a long discussion on his golfing equipment. I noticed that he was a little like me in practice. He was not bothered by his score. All that mattered was getting to know the course.

After that interlude, the course I then had to get to know was Royal Lytham and St Annes. It was the scene from 21–26 July of the 45th English Amateur Championship and I was intent on being around on the 26th. There is nothing dramatic about Royal Lytham because, unlike most of the other leading links courses, it is tucked away in rather an urban setting. In fact, it is considered by some experts to be a seaside course rather than a links. But there is one thing that all golfers agree upon . . . Royal Lytham and St Annes provides one of the sternest tests of golf in the world.

Mark James, a member of our Walker Cup side that year, provided the first shock of the week. He was the defending champion but he was on his way back home to Lincolnshire after being beaten in the opening round on the 18th green by Brian Stockdale. I had a comparatively easy first match against R. Pritchard, a left-hander from Coventry, and I went through 3 and 2. By coincidence I also had to beat another left-hander – Philip Morley – in the semi-finals, but before that I survived a heart-stopping moment in the fifth round and a tough quarter-final encounter.

Brian Winteridge, a 25-year-old from Stoneham, gave me the fright of my life in the fifth round. I was 1 up when we came to the 162 yard 9th and I reasoned that if I could win the hole and double my advantage, it would pressure him into making mistakes over the back 9. I struck a solid shot and it left me with a rather long but nevertheless sinkable birdie putt. Then Brian took out his nine-iron and punched the ball at the green. I thought I was seeing things when the ball hit the flagstick and dropped straight into the hole. It was an incredible way to square the match, but I had already told myself that it was going to be a hard slog. So I got my head down and I eventually won through by 2 holes after Brian had trouble with the bunkers at the 18th. The only sad part about that day was that the prospect of an all-Welwyn Garden City final disappeared when my clubmate Chris Allen was beaten at the 21st hole by Reg Glading, who at 49 was the oldest scratch golfer in Britain.

Gordon Edwards, from the Wirral, presented a real threat in the quarter-finals. He had been putting like a genius all week and twice he holed long ones on the front 9 as our match see-sawed. Then he made two more good putts at the 12th and 13th and edged 1 up. There is not a lot you can do when your opponent is holing the putts from all over the place and although I squared by winning the 14th I knew he was capable of slotting home a putt at any time and putting the pressure back on me. But, as luck would have it for me, he missed a short one at the 15th and I boomed a monster drive down the 17th to set up a 2 and 1 win.

It meant that Philip Morley and I, who had been sharing the same lodgings throughout the week, faced each other in the semi-finals. Philip was being hailed as the best left-hander in Britain since the arrival of Peter Dawson, runner-up in the English Amateur in 1969 and now a professional. Philip had plenty of ambition. 'I want to become the second left-hander to win the Open Championship,' he declared boldly – New Zealander Bob Charles was the first in 1963, also at Royal Lytham. Our match did not turn out to be a classic, because I won by the comfortable margin of 4 and 3. But it did have one moment best forgotten for when we arrived at the 10th green we found the hole filled with sand and the flag forced into the dummy hole which had been cut for the final the next day. It seemed vandals had been at play, but after a short delay we continued on our way.

The final of the English Amateur is over 36 holes and, although Gary Player would maintain that in match-play the game is far from finished until the final putt has dropped, I reckoned the title was mine after the first 18 holes. For against David Eccleston, a 27-year-old Lancashire golfer, I went into lunch 6 up after completing the course in 69 strokes. I think the last 3 holes really hurt David because I holed from over 10 feet at the 16th and 17th to win both with birdies and he lost a chance of taking the 18th by 3 putting. Nevertheless he refused to let me have things all my own way in the afternoon and the match did not finish until the 32nd green.

It was a fantastic moment. I was the 1975 English Amateur Champion. And I had made history by becoming the youngest player to ever win the championship. Surrey's Warren Humphreys was the youngest before me – he had been 19 when he took the title in 1971. But I was only nine days past my 18th birthday. Former Walker Cup Captain Gerald Micklem commented, 'Well done, my boy. But I thought it was next year you were going to win everything.'

The Sunday papers made good reading. Dudley Doust commented in the *Sunday Times* that of many spectacular protégés in British golf, few could have made a more mercurial rise than Faldo has done.

Pat Ward-Thomas in the *Guardian* on the Monday wrote that, in the past ten years or so, Oosterhuis alone had fulfilled early promise. 'But Nick Faldo, of Welwyn Garden City, could be another,' he went on. 'It would be surprising if this success was a sudden flash of glory because there is a distinct quality of the unusual about Faldo. The exceptional strength of his wooden and iron play would stand favourably in any company, and is achieved with less effort than I have seen in any young golfer for many years. This plainly is a natural gift. For a boy his approach to the game is uncommonly mature.'

I said to the golf correspondents at the time that I did not consider myself ready to take the knocks and reverses of pro golf, and I meant exactly what I said. I was not concealing any desire to turn to the paid ranks – even though out of the £108 I took with me to Royal Lytham I managed to return home with only a tenner. For I truly hoped, in Mr Ward-Thomas's words, to be a heartening example to amateur golf and maintain my status so that I would be available for the Walker Cup in two years' time.

But golf, like life, changes as often as the tide. I had started
the year of 1975 with the ambition of winning the Carris
Trophy – one of the top boys' competitions over the Moor
Park course, where later I lost that confrontation with Seve
Ballesteros. Yet in that event I took 86 in the second round.
Two weeks after my English Amateur triumph I had won the
British Youths Championship at Pannal in Yorkshire. Next, I
was representing my country. The press called it a meteoric
rise. For me it meant going back to school!

5

Space City

At the age of 18 I had decided to take an ambitious and exciting step which meant going to school 3000 miles away across the Atlantic. I was one of three young and promising amateurs – Sandy Lyle and Martin Poxon were the other two – to enrol in the January of 1976 on a golf scholarship at the University of Houston in Texas. The university dates back to 1934 but Houston itself was founded in 1836 and takes its name from General Sam Houston who won Texan independence from Mexico. But I soon found out that they called Houston 'Space City' because of the close proximity of the Manned Space Centre. It turned out to be a rather apt name because Sandy and I caused a few explosions of our own.

Sandy turned his back on America when his university entrance examinations failed to come up to expectations. He was told he must go to the nearby junior college while waiting for the opportunity to transfer to the University of Houston later on. I know for certain that Sandy was not very partial to that idea. He didn't feel like being separated from Martin and me. We had all gone there together and Martin and Sandy were already good friends and if they were going to be in Houston they wanted to be at the same place. But it was not to be and Sandy returned home to Hawkstone Park in Shropshire.

Six weeks after Sandy left, I also returned home. Dave Williams, the golf coach at Houston, had said, 'Nick's got a lot of potential. He's long enough off the tee but he needs lots of competition. Technically I think his swing is a little loose. He's got to get firmer.' But I was not happy with things at

Houston and I didn't feel that I was being given enough time to improve my golf.

There was simply too much studying. We spent three hours in the classroom every morning. I was missing the usual practice sessions I had at home. I was used to hitting 600 practice shots a day. I had been doing that for three years and I was now being asked to break my routine. It naturally led to a deterioration in my game. We also had no freedom. I didn't have my own transport and so had to ask for a lift to the nearest practice ground which was twenty minutes away. This was only 220 yards long and extremely narrow. If four players went there together it was inevitable that two of them would want to go back to the digs before the others and so all had to return as a party. It didn't suit my loner image. Driving ranges were good but the bags of balls were expensive. And they were all surlyn-covered Top Flites. Well, you can stand there all day hitting those and you will think that you have got it. But it doesn't turn out that you have !

I did get an insight, however, into how good the American courses are. We were close to Woodlands, a course where that year Lee Elder, the black American golfer, won the Houston Open. Only three years later I was to beat Elder in a Ryder Cup singles match. The course was fantastic, with its outrageous jigsaw-shaped bunkers. Playing at Woodlands provided an opportunity to test my golf and I was far from happy with the results.

After only two weeks at university I began to think that the pattern of the week's schedule was wrong. And I couldn't see it changing. We had to study all the time. If we went to play in an event it was a case of studying to catch up lost time. And you had to do the studies to remain in the university to obtain a scholarship. It was necessary to maintain a 70 per cent pass rate.

From the second week to the fifth week I hardly got a chance to go and hit shots. All we did was go out on practice rounds. That is no way to improve your game. The coach said I wasn't striking the ball quite right and he still wanted me to go out on the course and try to correct the faults. It seemed to me that the only thing in which they were really interested was your putting. If you could hole the putts you were all right. It was

the first question I had been asked, 'Are you a good putter?'
Even the basketball coach questioned me on my putting ability!

Dave Williams, the golf coach, has been at the University
of Houston for twenty-five years. I'm sure that he is one of
the most successful coaches in America. But he is not a teacher
and he openly admits that he does not like getting too heavily
involved on the technical side. If we had a problem it was a
case of going to an outside professional and paying for it. I was
on a partial scholarship, which meant that I was being given
my books, tuition and accommodation and I also got my meals
free. It was worth almost £500, and so I could have no complaints on that score. But I objected to having to pay for a
professional to give me advice. That was ridiculous when you
were there to learn golf. In the end I think the boys tried to
sort out each other's games.

At the same time we had to retain a razor-sharp edge. We
were all competing to earn places in the six-man Houston team.
In the first match I got in at number five and we went into
action against tough opposition from Southern Methodist
University, Texas A and M and Texas University. Ben Crenshaw had been to the University of Texas and he made a bit
of a name for himself by winning the National Collegiate
Championship on three successive occasions.

The matches are played over 36 holes, with the aggregate
scores of the top four players counting. We won by 760 to 771
but more important for me was that after scoring 81 in the
opening round, when the wind blew at up to 50 m.p.h., I went
out again to card a solid 74. It meant that I was joint ninth
in the individual tournament and third in my team. So I was
exempt for the next match and I wouldn't need to take part
in the regular pre-qualifying tests, sometimes played over as
many as four rounds, to see who was moving up into the team.

Houston could be a fun place. With more than 35,000
students on the campus, it is not too hard to find a few friends
and enjoy oneself. If you are an amateur golfer and you want
to study, there is probably nowhere better to go. But I think
it is necessary to be aware of the general routine out there. I
am glad that I went to America at that time in my life because
I did learn that I could go back and live in the country. But after
six weeks I had to get away, because in my opinion the short-

sighted golfing programme was doing nothing for my game. I could feel Space City closing in on me. So I quit.

For the first time since I took up golf, I could feel my game slipping away. I was losing my ability to produce the shots which had brought me so much success in 1975. My whole life was being put out of gear by the Houston timetable and the limited opportunities to practise was beginning to get me down. My game was going and I could see no hope of it returning to normal unless I returned home and sorted myself out. I was in America for a total of ten weeks and in that time I had ten practice sessions. When I compared that with my routine at home I knew I was in the wrong place. I had always practised in the morning and played a round in the afternoon. It was a successful formula for me.

When I stepped off the plane back home, I knew I had made the right decision. Yet I was criticized in the newspapers for my decision. Some of the comments were quite biting. Dudley Doust, in the *Sunday Times*, wrote, 'Faldo, a prodigy, is suffering a disease common to so many British golfers, both amateur and professional; things have come too easily for him. He was, perhaps still is, a glorious prospect . . . He has come out of it poorly and, as the reigning English Champion, doubtless has left a bad taste behind him.'

The headline proclaimed: NO FAIRWAY FOR FALDO'S FOLLIES.

It hurt. But I didn't complain. I had my own point of view and I decided there and then that I would prove – quickly! – that I had made the right decision. In fact it was a little more than one year later that Dudley, previewing the 1977 Open Championship at Turnberry, wrote that the young home player who had made the most progress over the last couple of years had been Nick Faldo. He added, 'Writers, notably myself, were rough on Faldo for quitting his golf scholarship at the University of Houston in the spring of 1976, but, so far, he seems to have vindicated his decision to turn professional.'

Before I had left Houston I had already cabled my father to get the entry forms for the early events on the amateur circuit. I was looking forward, among other things, to playing in the Lytham Trophy at the beginning of May because the previous year I had been balloted out because my handicap – 3 at the time – was too high. Of course, I did manage to get to Royal Lytham and St Annes a little later that year . . . and won the English Amateur.

I arrived home on 14 March and so there were other events before the Lytham tournament in which to play. Almost exactly one month later I travelled to the first of them – for a tournament which should have been the curtain-raiser to my 1976 amateur programme. Instead it turned out to be the last amateur event in which I competed, for I surprised the golfing world by turning professional. I went to Scotland for the King George IV Trophy at Craigmillar Park. It was my first opportunity of proving to others – I had no need to prove anything to myself – that I was right in returning from Houston. I reeled off rounds of 68, 70, 76 and 68 and my aggregate of 282 was 4 strokes better than runner-up George Macgregor.

It was something about that win which convinced me that I should not stay around as an amateur with the aim of winning a place in the Walker Cup in 1977. I turned professional purely because of ambition. I needed a challenge and I had decided that amateur golf could not provide me with enough fuel for my insatiable hunger for success. I had climbed a mountain by becoming the number one amateur in 1975. Now I knew that a switch to the professional ranks would take me back to the bottom rung of the ladder. But that was what I wanted. Though not for long!

6

Cheers, Skol

My first professional tournament was the French Open at Le Touquet from 6–9 May – and I went into it with some sound, if unexpected, advice from American player Ben Crenshaw. His message was, 'Tell that boy to go out and win the French Open, and set his sights no lower.'

Ben's words helped me to realize at the start of my professional career that I could set my sights higher. He was asked for his opinion on me by Ben Wright, golf correspondent of the *Financial Times*, after I had told another golf writer that I had been advised to set myself small targets, and I had continued, 'If I pre-qualify I see it as the equivalent of winning a one-day amateur tournament. If I get through to the last day of a pro tournament it will be equal to winning the English Amateur Championship again.'

Crenshaw, in his first appearance after winning his player's card for the US PGA Tour, had won the San Antonio Open in 1973, and he now told Ben Wright, 'I had been confident of making the cut at San Antonio, which was important. But even more vital was my thinking that during and after the qualifying school I had played the kind of golf that was good enough to win a professional tournament if only I could reproduce it. Faldo must know that too. There was absolutely no pressure on me in my first professional tournament, and Faldo should realize this. He should go out and play for his life before he starts to realize, as I did, the enormity of his achievement. Maybe he will suffer the kind of relapse that hit me when I was stupid enough to start thinking that the game that had served me so well as an amateur was not good enough technically for the professional game. But he must know and believe he can win in France and think of nothing else until he has done so.'

In fact, I finished joint thirty-eighth at Le Touquet – it was to be two years before I really broke through by winning the Colgate PGA Championship. But Ben's words helped me to realize I could set my sights higher. I suppose I was trying to remain level-headed following the events of the previous few weeks, but to be truthful I inwardly felt what Ben Crenshaw had said was true. I was aiming for the top.

I had to wait for my first tournament success until August 1977, in the Skol Lager 36 hole Individual event at Gleneagles, one of Scotland's most beautiful golfing centres. It came three weeks before my Ryder Cup appearance. Two weeks after the Ryder Cup I gained another victory when I won the Laurent Perrier Trophy, an eight-man invitational event, in Belgium. The latter tournament was played over 54 holes and so at the end of 1977 it was correctly pointed out that I had still to prove myself capable of withstanding intense pressure and winning a fully fledged 72 hole contest.

Still, the Skol was a notable moment in my life. It was my first professional victory and it brought with it a cheque for £4000. I was, in soccer jargon, over the moon. Yet when I look back I still find it a little difficult to believe that I won the Skol. I arrived at Gleneagles feeling in the right frame of mind because my place in the Ryder Cup was assured. So I no longer had any worries on that score. But I 3 putted the 1st hole of the King's course, and I thought there and then that it was just going to be a valuable warm-up for the Double Diamond World Golf Classic, which was to be played over the same course immediately following the Skol.

I was a member of England's five-man team and I was really looking forward to facing the crack American side, which included Lee Trevino and Jerry Pate, both former US Open Champions. It seemed likely to be a good test before the Ryder Cup. As it turned out, England finished bottom in Group One, we were eliminated, and the only opponents I played against were Australian Ian Stanley and Kazuo Yoshikawa from Japan. And I lost to both of them.

In fact, I played quite nicely against both Stanley and Yoshikawa, better than I played in the curtain-raising Skol event. Yet I won the Skol when I felt my game was nothing special. It is a strange story which you will hear time and time again from golfers. Sometimes you play well and return only moderate scores. On other occasions, you look really rusty, but you perform well. It just happens to work out that way.

I suppose the majority of the field in the Skol were given a boost when the Americans arrived at Gleneagles, without their clubs. They had been lost in transit. So the rest of us mere mortals had a psychological advantage over the likes of Trevino and Pate. And I reckoned we needed it. In the first round I seemed to plod round the course, the touch paper flickering but refusing to ignite, but I finished with a 2 under par 68 and that was surprisingly good enough to share the lead with Ernesto Acosta of Mexico.

Acosta had won the Individual title in the World Cup in 1976 in America and he was making his first tour of Europe. The smiling face behind a pair of tinted-lens glasses and buried underneath a peaked golfing hat had already become popular with spectators and there was a graveyard hush as poor Ernesto proceeded to run up a nightmarish 10 at the 2nd hole in the second round. Those who continued to file along the fairways and through the purple heather and golden gorse with Acosta witnessed a remarkable recovery. He bravely fought his way back to finish with 73. But he was not to be involved in the finish. Brian Barnes went to the other extreme and he put together an incredible course record of 63, but neither was that to be enough – in the first round he had taken 79 and earned himself a fine of £250 for playing the last hole one-handed!

So there can be little doubt that the Skol was one of those events. The Americans had lost their clubs; the joint leader had taken a 10; Barnes had first entertained the crowd with his own on-the-spot game and then demonstrated his natural talent with a scorching round. Me? I just kept plodding along, unsure what the exact situation was and cushioned only by the knowledge that nobody, except Barnes, was making a significant run. It was at the 17th that I learned I needed to par my way in to force a play-off. Welshman Craig Defoy, a superbly gifted player, whose true talent has never really been rewarded, produced a best of the day 67 to settle on the 139 mark with Australian Chris Witcher. I needed to hole from 4 feet to get the first par out of the way but just as I was about to putt my concentration was broken by a BBC jeep coming down a hill 'on the brakes'. The driver could see I was putting but he kept coming and the screeching and squealing shattered the silence. I went to putt three times and three times I backed away. Then I decided I just had to hit the damn thing – and I missed.

I was not a very happy individual. I stormed to the next tee. In temper, I ended by thrashing the ball on to the green. This was not the cool, calm Nick Faldo that everybody thought had joined the professional ranks. Here was an irate young man, steaming mad at what had happened and now doubly determined to win the Skol. For the first time in two days it had come home to me that I could win. And nothing was going to stop me. I faced up to a 30 yard eagle putt intent on holding it and winning outright. I struck the ball firm and true. It raced towards the hole, dropped . . . and I raised my arms in sheer delight. But the crowd were making the wrong kind of noises and out of the corner of my eye I could see that the ball had popped out again and the tournament was far from over.

Even so, I was in a play-off and I knew that victory was going to be mine. I boomed a super drive up the first extra hole and my approach finished 8 feet from the flag – inside both Defoy and Witcher. They both putted up and missed and I was left with an 8 foot putt for my win. It was not as easy as that, because it was straight downhill and if you went back to the first green now and took a look you would see that I only had two chances. The first was for the ball to go in, the second was for it to miss and carry on picking up speed and finishing outside both Defoy and Witcher. It looked like heads I win or tails I lose. In fact Craig, a great chap, laughed about it afterwards because he said that I never had a hope in hell of missing. He said that he was looking at me and he knew I was going to hit it straight into the back of the cup. Craig reckoned that most players in those circumstances would send the ball away with a touch start and sit back and hope that it curled into the hole. But he said that he could see that I was so determined that I would just take aim and fire. That is what I did and the Skol was mine. Winning meant more to me than anything else. The £4000 cheque for a couple of days' play was a case of nice

work if you can get it. But this was my first success and I
cherish the moment.

The Laurent Perrier in Belgium in September was a completely different affair. It was played at the Royal Waterloo
Club, to which Henry Cotton had been attached when he
won the first of his three Open titles in 1934, and it involved
only eight players. The tournament had been instigated in
memory of Donald Swaelens, the professional of the club, who
had died a year or so earlier while still in his thirties. We were
playing in the shadow of Wellington's defeat of Napoleon and
for me the pressure was great because I was Britain's only repre-
sentative, the others being Americans Hale Irwin, Billy Casper
and Bill Sander, Mexican Ernesto Acosta, Italian Baldo Dassu,
Belgian Philippe Toussaint and . . . Seve Ballesteros from
Spain.

This was my first chance to meet head-to-head with Seve and
gain revenge for my defeat in the Uniroyal. I was oozing with
confidence, following the euphoria of the Ryder Cup, and I
knew the press and the public were watching with interest to
see how I was going to develop. I was determined not to let
anybody down – least of all myself. My game was good and
so I was not surprised that I was able to put together a couple
of opening 69s. Since this was a 54 hole event it meant I went
into the final round with a 1 stroke lead over the experienced
Casper and a 2 stroke advantage on Seve.

What did surprise me was the arrival on the Sunday of the
British press. They seemed to be taken by the situation and
they came over, I suppose looking back, to build up the battle
between Nick Faldo and Seve Ballesteros. I was glad I was
able to give them something to write about.

Seve and I were paired together – and what a start! Seve
unleashed a typical opening rush with two birdies and an
eagle in the first 4 holes. I should have been shaken, especially
when I learned that Casper had started with two birdies, but
I was beginning to learn how to handle difficult moments such
as this, and I let Seve see that this was not going to be a walk-
over. I struck back. I reached the turn in 35, nothing fancy but
good enough to give me a 1 stroke lead over Seve, and with
Casper dropping back I reckoned my chances were better than
good. Seve soon put a stop to that way of thinking. He birdied

45

both the 10th and the 11th to forge ahead and I knew I had a battle on my hands.

But the 13th proved unlucky for Seve as he paid the penalty for trying to cut the corner at this dog-legged hole. He thumped his drive into the thick forest and the ball was lost. It meant he had to return to the tee and play – his third strike. It led to a 6 and my cast-iron par 4 gave me a 1 stroke lead again. I was 2 ahead after the next where Seve sent another drive spinning into trouble. At the 17th it was my turn to be confronted with a problem. I struck my second into a rhododendron bush. But I managed to hack it out on to the green and I holed a goodish putt and really that was that. I banked another £4000 and I returned home a happy man.

The next morning I was astonished at the praise from the press. I realized I had gone from beating Nicklaus and Watson in the Ryder Cup to taking on and cutting down Seve, the new pride of European golf. But I couldn't believe the amount of exposure my win in Belgium got in the papers. It was incredible. Michael McDonnell, writing in the *Daily Mail*, said, 'His display was not only thrilling but also showed clear evidence that he is the stuff of champions.' Afterwards I thanked him and the other writers for coming across the Channel to watch the finish. They seemed slightly surprised that I should make such a gesture but I was truly flattered that they had made the effort.

I have to admit that I was also flattered by the comments of Billy Casper, who finished second with Seve. He told Peter Ryde, golf correspondent of *The Times*, 'Nick has more talent than anyone I have seen out of Britain. I would like him to get to the States . . . he gets a little hot when he misses a shot, but that's youth.'

I felt tremendous. The headline in the *Daily Express* read: FABULOUS FALDO . . . NICK GUNS DOWN THE GIANTS AGAIN IN BATTLE OF WATERLOO.

And in the *Daily Mail*: FALDO HAS THE CLASS TO RULE EUROPE FOR YEARS.

I managed to bring myself down to earth by remembering that I had still not won a 72 hole tournament. That had to be my next target and so the Colgate PGA Championship at Royal Birkdale in 1978 was really the 'Big One'.

7
The Big One

The front page of the *Daily Express* on 30 May 1978 gave a true reflection of the heatwave Britain was experiencing. It described the weather as 'incredible'. I woke up to read the papers that morning feeling pretty much the same. In fact I felt absolutely fantastic . . . in spite of driving home to Hertfordshire down the motorway during the night following a late supper in Southport's Prince of Wales Hotel. About fourteen hours earlier I had won the Colgate PGA Championship.

If the attention that the press gave me a few months earlier in Belgium was unbelievable, then the 'notices' that I received the morning after my win over the Royal Birkdale Links were astonishing. The lead story in the same edition of the *Daily Express* read, 'Sunnyside Up! Britain is suddenly sizzling with success, lit up by two dazzling young sports stars. Swimmer Sharron Davies and golfer Nick Faldo hit the heights yesterday. Ice-cool Nick emerged as Britain's newest and most exciting golf champion clinching the £10,000 Colgate PGA title. He won by seven shots.'

It was almost too much to believe. I had to keep pinching myself that I was £10,000 richer. But I had the cheque and I knew that I had arrived.

I had arranged with my father that if I won he should make sure that there was a case of champagne in the press tent. I wanted to show my gratitude to the golf writers for the support they had given me. I wanted to share my moment of joy with them. Relationships with the press can be strained on occasions; but everybody in the tent that evening at dusty

Royal Birkdale was bubbling. It also gave them a story – Mark Wilson of the *Daily Express* commenting next day that I had shown 'the five-star class of Walter Hagen and the late Tony Lema in celebrating victory by calling for champagne'.

There were similar glowing tributes in the other morning newspapers, and I especially liked the words of Michael McDonnell in the *Daily Mail* referring to the new breed of young professionals: 'What sets Faldo apart from all of them is his gift of making it all look so damnably easy.' In a manner of speaking, it captured my own feelings throughout the week.

From the moment I had arrived in Southport I had this almost eerie presence: a realization that the time had come for me to win a 72 hole tournament. I cannot explain how it came about, for on arriving at Royal Birkdale I was more than a little depressed. Not only had I finished second again to Seve Ballesteros in the Martini International the previous week but now the weather had turned sour.

It was an appalling day on the Tuesday when I set off very early for my first practice round over the demanding 7001 yard Lancashire links. I remember hitting two drivers at the 1st and still not reaching the green. So it seemed probable that it was going to be a very tough week because Royal Birkdale is the kind of course where you can be severely punished if you miss the greens. And the longer the second shots you need to hit the more difficult it is to find the putting surface in the regulation number of strokes. I also had my worst suspicions confirmed when I finished that opening practice round and went over for a chat with the boys in the PGA caravan. It seemed that this was the most hazardous wind, because it usually meant that bad weather was on the way.

As it worked out, it could not have been further from the truth. When we arrived for the first round on the Friday morning the weather had cleared. It was a marvellous day and I felt really in the mood. In the mood to go and challenge for a title which could change my life and confirm that my youthful potential could be realized.

When I arrived on the 1st tee I felt tremendous. Hugh Baiocchi, the South African golfer who has made a habit of winning tournaments on the Continent, was one of my partners. That was a bit of a boost, because Hugh is one of the easiest-

Two triumphs to remember for the rest of my life – I shake hands with Gary Player after winning a challenge match at Welwyn Garden City, my home course, and (below) with Tom Watson after successfully keeping my 100 per cent record in the 1977 Ryder Cup.

Practice makes perfect – I keep my bunker game in shape in the back garden of my Hertfordshire home.

marry Melanie Rockall. From left to right: John Simpson, Dad, Mum,
myself and Mels, Melanie's Mum and Dad and bridesmaids Penny
Rockall, Jennifer Martin and Emma Wilson.

Dad, Mum and me at Wentworth for the Colgate World Match Play
Championships.

Barry Willett, a master at his craft, regularly checks my clubs at his
St George's Hill professional shop in Weybridge, Surrey.

going guys on the tour. He rarely gets flustered on the course and therefore you know that nothing he does will destroy your own concentration. I was also happy because in practice my game had been getting sharper and sharper and I was sure I had the course worked out well in my mind. It makes you feel so much better to go into an event when you possess an inner belief that you can handle the track.

What happened on the 1st hole I shall never forget as long as I live. I had made up my mind to hit a three-wood off the 1st tee, even though I realized it would need a positive shot with a long iron to reach the green with my second. In fact, I went with a two-iron and it was something about that shot which told me I was going to win the Colgate. Although it did not finish as close to the flag as I hoped at the time, I knew it was a perfect shot. I had an altogether different feeling inside me. I think it came about because I had willed myself into hitting a specific shot. I wanted to hit a high fade with that two-iron and it came off to perfection. Even if you play the game for a living it gives you tremendous satisfaction to call a shot to yourself and execute it in the right way.

That one shot gave me the confidence to settle down and to play the front 9 in level par. In my opinion the secret of overcoming Royal Birkdale is in warming the engine over the first half in order that you don't make any mistakes, and then firing on all cylinders on the back 9. But on that first day there was a slight hiccup in this driver's planning. I took 7 down the 17th. Yet it failed to ruin my concentration and when I reached the tee at the 18th I felt calm and assured that I could get a shot back at the last with a birdie. It worked out just that way and Gerald Micklem walked over to me at the end and he said, 'I'm glad you made that birdie. It showed a bit of courage and it gives you something to go at tomorrow.'

To the modern-day golfing public the name Gerald Micklem might mean very little. But to me and to many other golfers Gerald has been a valued spectator, a fine friend and a person to whom one would look for guidance. In fact, he is one of the game's foremost administrators and during his own playing days he was a top amateur golfer. He won the English Amateur title in 1947 and 1953 and he was a member of the Walker Cup team on four occasions, captaining the side in 1957 and

1959. As an administrator Gerald is much respected and, among many positions he has held, he has been Chairman of the Rules of Golf Committee, the Royal and Ancient Championship Committee and an R and A Selection Committee, Captain of the Royal and Ancient Golf Club, and President of the English Golf Union and of the European Golf Association. So I deem myself fortunate that he often followed my golf game as an amateur and that he was on the spot at the Colgate to give me a few words of encouragement at the end of the first round.

In fact, I was only 3 shots off the pace. The leader after the first round was South African Dale Hayes. After two unhappy years playing in America, Dale had elected to return to Europe where he had finished top of the Order of Merit in 1975. It was soon apparent that he had made the right decision because in the three weeks leading up to the Colgate he had won the Italian Open by 3 shots, the French Open by 11 shots and he had finished fourth in the Martini International. So after shooting a first-round 68 at Royal Birkdale he must have had thoughts of a third win in four weeks. He led by one stroke from Seve and three British players, Peter Townsend, John Hammond and Garry Cullen. That hooked shot to the 17th and an unplayable lie had led to a 71 for me.

I was out late on the second day. Again it was a beautiful morning and by the time I arrived at the course I fully expected to see the leader board bunched with a galaxy of names all well under par. But exactly the opposite had occurred. Seve slid to a crunching 79. Dale crashed to 76. Garry Cullen also took 76 and poor John Hammond frittered away his hopes with 80. I knew that if I could play well I would shoot right through the field ... perhaps to the top.

Yet that second round, which eventually took me to the front and set up my first big win, was one of the most extraordinary affairs of my life. I covered the first 9 holes in level par and I felt good. Then I began to feel a certain chilliness on my arms. I thought to myself, 'Surely I can't be getting nervous at this stage!' But I was so cocooned in concentration that I had neglected to notice the sea mist rolling across the course and turning a golden afternoon into a grey, autumn-like picture. It was quite dramatic. In such circumstances one often questions the wisdom of continuing. Both Hugh and I were having trouble spotting each other, on occasions, on either side of the fairways. So seeing the green and imagining the shot to be played was an experience which few would desire. For me, however, it made no difference to my outlook. I seemed to be so convinced that this was to be my week that I was unwilling to allow the changing circumstances to destroy my relentless progress around the course that Saturday afternoon.

I can remember standing on the 13th fairway and realizing that it was possible for me to lead. So I made a firm commitment to continue. Those who know the 13th hole will appreciate it is not one at which to take a gamble. There are trees and bushes down the left-hand side and I had a wood in my hand trying to hit the green in 2 and set up the prospect of an eagle. At the same time, the mist was swirling all around and I couldn't see the green. Then the mist drifted off the green for a few seconds and I made up my mind to go for glory or disaster. I was level par, I had been waiting for three minutes to catch a glimpse of that green. My view was still slightly blurred but I knew this was the moment that fate had sent to test my courage.

I struck that three-wood with a blinding flash. As the ball sailed through the air the mist was already coming down again on the green. But it held back just enough to allow me to see the ball hit that lovely green grass. It finished 30 feet from the hole and I sank the putt for an eagle 3. Gene Kelly may have enjoyed 'Singing in the Rain' but I can tell you I felt at that moment like dancing in the mist. In my opinion that shot won me the Colgate PGA Championship.

I did drop a shot at the next hole, the short 14th, but I birdied the 15th, in spite of being disturbed on the tee when I was about to drive. The mist was even worse at the 17th and 18th, the two par 5s which complete the Royal Birkdale circuit, but I birdied both of them. It gave me a 68, a remarkable round in those circumstances, and I finished on 139 – 2 ahead of Peter Townsend and 5 clear of no fewer than eleven players gathered on the 144 mark.

Gerald Micklem came over and said my round ranked as one of the best six rounds he had ever witnessed. I was delighted by that and I returned to the Prince of Wales Hotel feeling pretty happy with life. When I got back I ran into one of the officials from Colgate and I went over to thank him for a remark he made over breakfast. He wandered over and simply said, 'Go on Nick, get out there and give them hell.' I never forgot that.

So the third day dawned and I was itching to get going. I was paired with Peter Townsend, one of those superb professionals who has never realized his full potential. Why he should not have won more titles puzzles more than me. For that third round I could hardly have wished for a better partner. Like Hugh Baiocchi, my partner for the first two days, he has admirable patience. And on top of that he has happy memories of Royal Birkdale. In 1968 he took the runner-up spot behind Gay Brewer in the Alcan Golfer of the Year and twelve months later he won three of his five Ryder Cup matches over the course.

Unfortunately Peter was to tumble back on the fourth and final day with an 82. But in the third round he produced a solid 72 which meant that I had to stay aware of the possibility of being overtaken. I was confident about remaining in front because my short game was in good order and if I missed the green I felt certain that I would get up and down in 2 to keep my momentum flowing. But I didn't give the spectators too much excitement over the first eleven holes. I made pars at each one and I was quite satisfied with that until I dropped a shot at the 12th. But instead of shaking me it made me more determined and I birdied 3 of the last 4 holes – the 15th, 17th and 18th, which are all par 5s.

Now I returned to the hotel grasping a 4 shot lead. It might sound a lot but any golfer will tell you that shots on a golf course can disappear faster than a rabbit in a magician's top hat. And I knew that Townsend and Howard Clark, my two closest challengers, and Hayes, only 1 shot further back, would be ready to strike if I started to make errors. In fact Clark was right on the spot, because I was paired with him for that final day. That season 'Clarkie' had made a tremendous start by winning the Portuguese and Madrid Opens, the first and third events on the European tour, and finishing second behind Brian Barnes in between in the Spanish Open. So I knew that Howard had that winning feeling and the press had already

heralded him as a star of the future. But I was determined not
to let my chance slip away.

Yet anyone watching must have thought quite differently
over the first 3 holes in that last round. To begin with I hit my
tee shot at the 1st too far right and I was faced with a distance
to the pin which required a three-iron but a lie which told me
that the ball was going to fly and it could be any club. I elected
to go down to a seven-iron but the ball still pitched through the
green and ran up a slope. It left me with a near impossible
chip and I felt relieved when I got it to 5 feet. But I missed the
putt and a shot had gone. Luckily Clark let me off the hook
because he 3 putted. If he had made a birdie there it might
have been a different story.

There were more problems ahead. At the third I missed a
2 foot putt. I don't know how it happened, but I stood there
and talked to myself. 'Gee-whiz,' I thought, 'you're not going
to throw it away now.' The 206 yard 4th brought a further
obstacle to negotiate. I hooked my tee shot 30 yards wide of
the green and Howard hit his with great authority to 14 feet
from the flag. I made a rather in-and-out chip which settled
12 feet from the cup and Howard applied the pressure by holing
for a birdie 2. I was now facing a dilemma. If I missed the putt
it would mean that all but one of my overnight 4 shot lead
would have been eroded. And we still had fourteen holes to
play. I had to go for the putt – but if I was too bold and the
ball ran past it could lead to a double-bogey 5. Clark would
be level with me. He would be bubbling; I would feel deflated.
I reached for my mallet putter. And from the moment I struck
the ball I knew it was going into the hole. I felt great. I knew
that putt had steadied me and that I could resume control of
the situation.

I didn't feel nervous and when Howard dropped shots at
the 5th and 6th and I holed from 3 and 10 feet to save my
pars I knew it was virtually all over. There were no leader
boards at that point of the course but I told myself that if I
made a birdie to go 5 clear of Clark it was doubtful whether
anybody else was going to be that close to me. At the short
7th I hit a punched seven-iron to 10 feet and I shut the
door on Howard by holing the putt for a real confidence-
boosting 2.

To this day I reckon 'Clarkie' tried a little bit of gamesmanship at the 8th. He called for a ruling. Yet, in my mind, it was obvious that he could take a drop because his ball was simply behind a scoreboard. The European Tournament Players Division have repeatedly tried to point out to players that they should know the rules well enough not to have to call for a tournament director's ruling if it is obvious what to do. But I think Howard wanted to make me wait and lose my momentum. We sat there for twenty minutes under a blazing sun, but there was no way it was going to make me mad.

Anyway, at that stage my nerves felt good and I knew that a 70 or thereabouts would ensure victory. And by the time I arrived at the 15th tee, which really meant that I couldn't get into much trouble, the boards were showing that I had a 5 shot lead and I could almost feel that £10,000 cheque in my sticky hands. And sticky was the operative word, because the heat and the tension of that tremendous afternoon in my life had combined to make my hands perspire much more than normal. I ended up by using no fewer than four gloves.

The only thing I didn't realize at the time was that as I arrived on the 15th tee Ken Brown was chipping into the cup from 60 feet at the 16th for his third birdie in succession, and in fact I held only a 3 shot advantage. But then it all started to happen for me. I hit a thumping drive down the 542 yard 15th, drilled a three-iron to 15 feet and rammed home the putt. It took me to 8 under and the best Brown could do was to finish with 70 and a 3 under par score of 285. It meant that the title was mine but I was determined to finish in the style of a thoroughbred horse winning a classic race. I reached the 17th green with two three-woods for a comfortable birdie 4, but at the last I wasn't quite certain what to do when I missed the green on the right with my second. I knew now I had it won but I wasn't certain how to treat the situation. I wondered whether I should do something to entertain the crowd and give people a laugh.

In the end I decided that it was best just to hit the ball and let it finish anywhere on the green. I could never 8 putt! In fact, I was left with a 10 footer. I hardly looked at the putt but the ball dived into the cup and the Colgate PGA Championship was mine. All mine.

It was a tremendous feeling. That was the big win that I had wanted. The one every golfer dreams about. And I had made it before my 21st birthday. I also knew that I had won in front of millions of TV viewers on a Bank Holiday Monday. That made it a little more special. The crowds cheered and Clark walked across the green to shake my hand and say, 'Congratulations'. That is a very sweet word.

The next minute I could hardly believe my eyes. This chap came almost falling off the small mound at the back of the green and zigzagged his way towards me. In one hand he had a glass and in the other held a bottle of champagne.

'Have a drink,' he murmured. I wondered what to do. Then I simply replied, 'Look, I must put my card in first.' I walked across to the PGA Caravan where we take the score cards to be officially signed and handed in. It was now that I began to shake. When you are concentrating on the course you don't have time to allow your emotions to reach inside you. Now I was beginning to understand what I had achieved. I sat in front of Bill Hodge, the official scorer, trying to add up the figures on my card. I couldn't get them to make much sense. I didn't even realize I had shot a 69, which meant that I had been the only player to break par in every round. Finally I knew everything was right and I signed the card. My last round of 69 had given me a total of 278 – 10 under par and 7 strokes ahead of my former Hertfordshire Colts team-mate Ken Brown. Howard had finished third with 73 for 286. It meant that the three young 'Brits' had called the tune.

I walked from the caravan and I saw my father. He didn't know what to say. Nor did I. It was one of those moments that you cherish forever – yet nothing was really said for a minute or two. Then I asked him to get the case of champagne into the press tent. I had to go and receive the trophy from David Foster, Colgate's chief executive.

I had an amusing tale to relate to Mr Foster. On arriving at the Prince of Wales Hotel at the start of the week I had asked for my room, only to learn one had not been reserved for me and the hotel was fully booked. So I went searching for Tim Kelly, who worked for Colgate and reminded him that I had booked a room through him in January, which he did not recall. However, I was proved right, and poor Tim had a problem as to where to put me. In the end he had only one option – David Foster was arriving a day late and so I had better use his suite for the evening. It was nice being chief executive of Colgate for a night – but it was even better being Colgate PGA Champion!

8
The Morning-After Feeling

After leaving the press tent that evening I surveyed the scene of my success. I suppose, unless you are a winner, it is rare for a player to see a course, like Royal Birkdale, after the 'Lord Mayor's show' is over. I looked around. For a few moments I realized that this lovely links layout, one of my own favourite courses, had actually belonged to me for a short while that afternoon. I think it is fair to say that, because people were watching my every move. And now, as the last stragglers made their way home, I couldn't help but feel the emotion of the moment. It was emotional saying goodbye to Royal Birkdale that evening.

We thought it would be nice to go back to the Prince of Wales for a meal before driving home. The hotel very kindly gave us a room in which to freshen up and my parents and I sat down to a celebration supper with James Erskine and Lisa Bratten, both from the International Management Group, and with Dale Hayes and his wife-to-be Linda. But we didn't want to stay for the evening and so I drove my parents back down the motorway and at three o'clock in the morning I was crawling into bed and the most momentous twenty-four hours of my life were over.

I had already elected to take the next week off and miss the British Airways/Avis Open in Jersey. So the next morning I could have lain in bed and dozed through to midday. But of course I wanted to see the newspapers and it didn't take me long to scan through all the populars and tell Mum to cut them out ready for the scrapbook. Then I was interested to read how the writers of the more serious papers had taken my win. All wrote very good reviews: Michael Williams in the *Daily Tele-*

graph revealed that I was the youngest British tournament winner since Bernard Gallacher, then 20, won the old Schweppes title at Ashburnham in 1969; and Pat Ward-Thomas in the *Guardian* said, 'It was probably the most commanding win ever by a young player in a British professional tournament.'

After the initial whirlwind of telephone calls from relatives, friends and colleagues and a few visits from the press, I was able to take things calmly that week. George Blumberg, over from South Africa, invited us to the Carlton Towers for dinner. He had been a great friend to me when I visited South Africa first as an amateur and then professional. I have to admit that it was staggering how I was being recognized out and about even at the Carlton Towers as well as in Welwyn Garden City when I went shopping. I suppose you always want people to know you, but suddenly it becomes rather embarrassing. I wasn't too sure whether I liked people peeking at me and wondering what I was up to. I wasn't a superstar; but the amount of press and television coverage had turned me into a familiar face. I needed to get back to reality.

The other important thing that I had to consider was my build-up for the Open Championship at St Andrews. That was little more than a month away and I realized that my win in the Colgate, seeing that it was on a links course, would mean that some of the game's experts would be labelling me as a potential Open Champion. It was a nice thought, but there were a few tournaments between now and the start of the world's oldest and greatest golfing event and I wanted to be sure that I gave my best in all of them.

Of course, I couldn't help starting to think about the Open and the prospect of emulating Tony Jacklin's brilliant win in 1969. It was a fact that in 1976, my first year as a professional, I had given a sign that I had the game for links courses by finishing with 69 to take joint twenty-eighth place in the Open alongside three star-studded names – Gary Player, Doug Sanders and Neil Coles. Ironically, that year the Open had been at Royal Birkdale, so you can gather that I have a certain affinity towards that course now. But one year later at Turnberry I had finished down the field as Tom Watson and Jack Nicklaus fought out that splendid battle which Watson so narrowly won. So even though I must admit that the thought of winning the Open in 1978 was very much in my mind, I knew that I had to get back to the grind of everyday tournaments and slowly raise myself 'up' for the big one. The next few weeks would be important for that and I was keen to ensure that I prepared properly.

My next tournament was in Brussels – scene of my win in the Laurent Perrier tournament the previous September – but on this occasion it was the Belgian Open and we were playing at the beautifully manicured Royal Golf Club of Belgium and not the Royal Waterloo course. Brussels is an expensive city and I remember thinking to myself that only two years earlier I would have had to hunt out the cheapest of places to eat and even then it would have stretched my pocket. Now, thankfully, I could afford the best meals and, although not wanting to throw money away, it does make the digestion system work better when you know it is not going to be a problem to pay the bill.

From a playing point of view, it was a rather straightforward week. I was in the groove and I opened with three successive 71s. It was nothing dramatic but it did mean that a good round on the last day might win for me the title. Alas, it was not to be and I finished with a rather ordinary 72 and in joint sixth place behind Australian Noel Ratcliffe, who produced a superb 66. For a time in Belgium it had seemed possible that either Ken Brown, who followed me home in the Colgate, or Tony Jacklin, would win. But Brown completely lost his game on the last day and he took 78. Jacklin also went backwards with 75. For Ken it was a clear chance missed to win his first tournament, but his breakthrough was to come later that same season. Poor Jacko, however, needed to wait more than another year before he ended a nightmare run of five years without a victory in a big event on the European circuit.

I was reasonably happy with my performance and it became more satisfying when I recalled that for thirteen successive rounds in competition I had not once scored over par. In fact twelve of them, beginning with a 69 in the last round of the French Open at La Baule on 15 May, had been sub-par scores. In the Martini I had reeled off 67, 70, 71 and 67 against a par of 71; in the Colgate my scores were 71, 68, 70 and 69 against a par of 72; and in Belgium the par was 73. So I was 29 under par for those thirteen rounds and that added up to an average of 2.23 under par a round. I would accept that every week!

Belgium was also a good week to get out of the way. My win in the Colgate had clearly created more interest with the press than I imagined. It was nice being the centre of attention, but my lifestyle was such that the arrival in Belgium of a news-gossip writer from the *Daily Mirror* momentarily upset my programme. I had to start talking about things other than golf – and at that time when I was at a tournament I allowed nothing to distract me from the game. When I got back from Belgium I picked up a copy of the *Sun* and there I was again – this time, would you believe, in the centre-page spread. I suppose I could be thankful that it wasn't page 3! Ann Buchanan, who wrote the article, hit the nail on the head when she said, 'He lives, sleeps and dreams golf. And he has that rare quality of believing you play to win.'

The next week I did come right back down to earth. I suppose some sort of reaction had to overtake me and in the Greater Manchester Open at Wilmslow I could only manage rounds of 74, 69, 77 and 75. But thoughts of the Open were now beginning to take preference over all other matters and I had already elected to miss the following week's Sumrie–Bournemouth tournament in order to take a rest.

I reckoned that the Sun-Alliance European Match-Play at the end of June would provide me with enough competition to sharpen my game before I went to St Andrews for the 108th Open.

In fact, I lasted only two rounds over the Dalmahoy course near Edinburgh. But in no way was I downhearted. In the first round against Peter Berry, who won the Mufulira Open in Zambia in 1978, I had a real peach of a day in spite of the fact that it was a bitterly cold and windy morning. Peter played the first 9 holes in 1 under par and I suppose, in those conditions, it would normally have been good enough to give him the lead in a run-of-the-mill match. But I turned 5 up after making four birdies in the first seven holes. I birdied the par 5 10th to go 7 under par and 6 up and, to make matters worse for poor Peter, I then holed a putt of 20 feet to get out of jail at the 13th and win the match 6 and 5.

The second-round match was even more dramatic. I was drawn to meet Garry Cullen. He had not won a cheque during the previous four weeks but he is a sound player and I knew our match could develop into a real battle. But in my wildest dreams I could never have foreseen the events of that extraordinary encounter.

This time I did not quite match my outward half of 30 on the previous day. But when I turned in 32 I knew I was beginning to wish it was a stroke-play event. I was scoring so well that I knew that nobody would have been capable of matching that kind of pace over 36 holes. It would have opened the way for me to sprint clear and to this day I still feel confident that if I had been playing in a 72 hole tournament that particular week I would have chalked up my second big win of the season. Instead I found myself out of the event that very evening.

Garry was also having a field day and it was a neck-and-neck affair. Looking back I think the turning point came at the 11th where I was just short in 2 and he had missed the green on the right. It seemed likely that I would get up and down in 2, but instead he chipped down to 4 feet and holed and I made a 5 to lose the hole. Then, at the 16th, I hit a drive for which I should not have been punished. It was only half a dozen feet off line but I couldn't even move it. Garry seized control, won the hole and he birdied the 17th to take the match 2 and 1.

So there I was, one moment going so well, but the next out of the event and on my way home. But that is the story so many times in match-play. It is a tough form of golf and we can often reflect how our golf might have been good enough to beat a number of competitors that same day. But you have to keep it in the mind that match-play concerns two people going head to head and only one can win.

There can also be only one winner of the Open Championship each year. And my next objective was to be that one.

9
Open '78

When superstars like Johnny Miller and Gary Player start talking golf you cock an ear. When they are talking about *you* then you make sure you don't miss a word they are saying. I had played with Johnny in the French Open earlier that year and surprisingly he had asked me for an impromptu lesson next to the 18th green at La Baule. Johnny was struggling to regain the game which had made him the golden boy of golf. I simply suggested that I felt he needed to work on a particular movement of his legs. Johnny said that, when he returned to his ranch in California, he would follow the advice. So it was a bit of a reward for me when he put together a couple of sub-70 rounds in the US Open a month later.

But I have to admit it was more rewarding to learn what Johnny thought of Nick Faldo. He told the press, 'You've got a British Open Champion here. The fellow can really play. He's a very talented golfer. You mark my words – he's going to the top.' Those words generated an enormous amount of confidence in me and, of course, it was only a couple of weeks later that I won the Colgate title.

Now the time had arrived for me to try to prove that Johnny Miller was right in tipping me as a future Open winner. The irony of it all was that I came to be paired in the first two rounds at St Andrews with Johnny. We were joined by Antonio Garrido of Spain.

But before setting off for the 'home of golf' I had a special date – with Gary Player. On the Friday of the previous week we were opponents in a £6000 winner-takes-all challenge match. And the venue was my own Welwyn Garden City course. It was a tremendous occasion for the club and I wanted to make it an even happier affair by beating Gary. What I achieved was almost beyond belief. Not only did I win the game, but I also shot a course record 65. It was a great warm-up – the best I could have hoped for – with the Open in mind and it was really terrific to get my hands on the course record at my local club.

Afterwards I listened to what Gary had to say about me. 'He's big and he's strong and he's got a nice swing. Now it is all just up to him. In today's golf world there are many potential winners and you can liken them to a stampede of racehorses coming to the last furlong. One can shoot out of the pack – and he's got the style to be the real thoroughbred.' They were words that I respected. And it sharpened my desire to show I could be first past the winning post.

Gerald Micklem had come along to Welwyn Garden City to watch the match. He was full of admiration at my performance, but he also realized that ahead was my first experience of St Andrews. Gerald had concluded that I might require a little assistance so he handed me three foolscap pages of notes detailing everything I needed to know about the 18 holes which make up the Old Course!

Gerald is a meticulous man, so I knew that I was fortunate to have his guide to the course. But when I read through the three pages I was bubbling with enthusiasm. It was better than an Ordnance Survey map. The detail was such that I felt I knew the Old Course like an old friend. Yet I had not even set out from home. And I had never set eyes on St Andrews. Gerald pinpointed every hump and hollow. He plotted the bunkers. He indicated where the pin positions would be. He wrote that, while it is generally assumed that the Old is a 'hooker's course', there are holes where it is necessary to be to the right in order to get the easier shot into the green. The only thing I could fault was his handwriting! It reminded me of the scrawl on a doctor's prescription. But I loved those 'doctors orders'.

I transferred Mr Micklem's invaluable notes to individual cards for each hole and John Moorhouse, my caddie, and I read them to each other as we took turns behind the wheel driving up the motorway to Scotland on the Saturday. We arrived at St Andrews at four o'clock in the afternoon, parked the car and hurried to take a first look at the course. I gasped at what I saw. I had seen the course on television, but until you have been to St Andrews you just cannot visualize it. Those huge greens made the heart pump really hard. This was something so different – and there was no time like the present for going out and finding how tough it was going to be.

But I resisted my first impulse to play the course. Instead, I simply walked out carrying a wedge club. John took a measuring wheel along to chart distances, but it was hardly necessary. We soon found out that Mr Micklem was absolutely spot-on with all his calculations. I was dumbfounded because he had sat at his desk at home and written out his notes. Yet every pot bunker was exactly located where he put it. The humps and the hollows were inch-perfect. And I was to discover as the week of the championship progressed that he was never far wrong with his pin placings.

Of course, he didn't have the holes in exactly the right spot. But he narrowed it down to certain sections of the greens. He suggested that on one day the pin would be placed behind a certain bunker and on another day it would be close to a particular slope in the green. He had marked a section on the second hole and on taking one look at the green I thought to myself that the championship committee would never put it there. But they did!

It was not only on the putting surfaces that Gerald helped me with. For instance, when you stand on the 1st tee at St Andrews you think to yourself, 'Ah, this is no problem. The fairway is more than 100 yards wide. What an easy way to start.' But Gerald pointed out that there was a line to take. It was 20 yards left of the green and it enables the golfer to have the optimum shot to the flag.

Throughout my short career Gerald Micklem has helped me a great deal. To some, his mere arrival close to a tee leads to disaster. He is much respected and I think because of that some young golfers tend to be put off when he is watching. But from an early stage in my amateur career – I think it was at the Boys' Championship in 1974 – he seemed to take an interest in my game and I became used to seeing him suddenly perching on his shooting-stick behind a green. Now I had the best advice he had ever given me: A guide to the Old Course.

He closed his comments on each hole with a superb summing up – 'You must never get mad at St Andrews. You must be willing to accept exactly what you get. Then you must keep on trying. Keep a clear mind all the time. For there are so many humps and hollows that it is easy to allow your mind to become tangled with frustration. Once you start seeking excuses, St Andrews has got you beat. It is no good saying that this or that is a silly hole. It is no good questioning why a hump should be here. Once you do that you can seriously forget your chances of winning. The Old Course must be treated sympathetically. Don't try to fight it, try to understand it. This applies to St Andrews more than perhaps 99 per cent of the courses I know in the world.'

It was sound advice. There were a lot of people who maintained that, because I had never seen St Andrews, I would never be able to play the Old Course in a low enough score to be involved in the championship. But Gerald's notes and my first round practice assured me that they would all be wrong. I was determined to obey the code and I felt that it was my kind of course. My confidence stemmed from the fact that he had also told me that St Andrews was the kind of course where you are often required to play little, half-punched shots. I worked hard on them. It meant, for instance, being able to go down the grip on a three-iron but using a full swing. The ball will often fly the same distance but it enables you to have more control. The ball flies lower and there is no fade or draw. There are occasions at St Andrews when that is of paramount importance.

Mr Micklem doubted whether I could use the shot in the Open itself with less than one week of practice. But I am always one for going in at the deep end and trying a new idea out in the actual tournament. I believe the only way one ever finds out whether or not one has actually captured the essence of a particular shot is by employing it under the most intense pressure. And there is nothing like the pressure of the Open for a golfer.

I went out for my first full practice round on the Sunday with Peter Townsend. I didn't discuss my notes with him and, for all I know, he might have also possessed a set because Gerald was a keen supporter of Peter when he came through as a leading amateur player in the sixties. I don't look to score in practice and so the Micklem 'pin-placing' chart gave me the chance to check the roll of the greens in the places where the holes were likely to be cut. So it might have seemed to the bystander when I was practising that my game was not exactly all together. This is because I made a point of aiming for where I had been told the pins could be placed. In some cases this meant aiming for a spot that was some distance away from the actual pin placings. But it was the only way to learn. I soon began to get a feel of the greens and I also made sure that I practised a few chip shots from improbable lies. That was in order that I was not caught out in the tournament if I hit a stray shot and subsequently faced a tough recovery.

On the Monday I met Hubert Green, who had won the United States Open the previous year. He was coming the other way, as we were on one of those double greens which are landmarks at St Andrews. He asked me if I wanted to play tomorrow and that sounded great. Then he told me that we would be forming a fourball with George Burns and . . . Tom Watson. Since I had beaten Tom in the Ryder Cup the previous year I was not too overawed. Nevertheless, it gave me a great kick to think that I would be practising for the 1978 Open with the defending champion. And I reckoned this was my chance to see if my game plan was right.

Tom Watson is a great thinker round a golf course. So I was interested to discover how he planned to play the Old Course. It was now Tuesday, the day before the Open was to begin, and I knew that Tom would be having his final work-out. He would be deciding exactly how he was going to play the 6933 yards layout. I left the course later that afternoon extremely encouraged. I had watched Tom closely and in my way of thinking he had done very little different from myself. He certainly had not devised any special methods to play certain holes. It was true he took a three-wood at the 1st whereas I took a driver, but basically he played for the same places. It made me feel great because I knew then and there that Tom Watson, twice Open champion, didn't have any secrets on me.

We finished that round about three o'clock. It gave me time to go over to the putting green. I stayed there for half an hour or so and then I went to practise my chipping. Finally I went to hit a few shots 'through the bag'. The Royal and Ancient had organized a driving area with range balls. There is nothing I like better, because it's great to be able to just stand there and hit a bag of balls away. It allows you to strike the perfect rhythm whereas when you are using a caddie to collect your balls it means that you have got to think all the time where he is standing. I prefer the freedom of being able to take out the driver and give it a swish. And it is much easier to change from driver to wedge because there is no need to wait for your caddie to get into another position.

I completed my practice and jumped in the car to drive back to Dundee. My mum, dad and I had been invited to stay for the week with Peggy McGregor, who once lived in Welwyn Garden City. My mother used to earn a few extra pennies by making dresses for Peggy. Then Peggy retired and she moved back to Dundee, where she had been born and bred. Originally I had been invited to stay with a group from Glynwed, the company to which I was attached, but they were not due to move into their house until the Monday of championship week and by the time they arrived I had settled in at Dundee. It was far enough from the course to be able to forget the pressures and close enough to get there in easy time by car. So I was happy to stay.

It needed to be close for the first round. Johnny Miller, Antonio Garrido and I had drawn an early start time – 8.10! But I was overjoyed with that. It meant that my starting time for the second round would be around 1.30 and not 3.30. The latter is a real killer because it means waiting around all day. And the good thing about an early time is that on the coast the conditions are quite often still in the morning, but then the breeze starts to get up and life can become more hazardous.

Five o'clock! The alarm shrilled in my ear. The Open was two and a half hours away from starting. I was due on the tee in three hours ten minutes. It was time to begin my preparation. It was cold and I ate a hearty breakfast. I dressed, making sure to put on my warmest and most comfortable roll-neck sweater, and I set off for the course. St Andrews is an ancient university city where, so some historians relate, golf was first played in 1552. It is grey and, when the weather is bad, very bleak. Yet it has become the mecca of golf and it was here that on 14 May 1754, twenty-two 'noblemen and gentlemen' got together to form the Royal and Ancient Club.

As I drove towards the town you couldn't but notice how the Open had completely taken over. The Open is no longer only about a golf course. The wings have spread and a huge tented village, where manufacturers promote and sell their goods, rises from the ground and dominates the scene. As you get closer the tap, tap, tap of hammers tells you that the workmen are putting final touches to the massive grandstands provided so that more than 100,000 people during the week will be able to view the golf in comfort.

The grandstands are necessities – but in my way of thinking they make the course easier! In my opinion they help to define the fairways. So do the ropes which run the length of the fairways so that the spectators remain on the walking routes chosen by the Championship Committee. The stands and the ropes and the people help to guide you to the green. I would sincerely love to play St Andrews with nobody else in view. For if you just stand on the tees it seems so innocent. But its prime protector, barring the ever-changing sea winds, is the fact that the fairways never seem to be there. You cannot define them with the naked eye. All you see are the humps. Of course, you know where the bunkers are placed, but not actually being able to see them makes everything so much tougher. I'm sure you could get lost!

Finally, I parked the car, put all my thoughts and dreams behind me and made my way to the practice green. It was seven o'clock. Momentarily my mind was turned away from the Open when I saw a huge transporter with a Ford Granada emblazoned with the words 'British Car Auctions'. BCA, whose managing director David Wickens is a golf fanatic, have supported several golfers by providing them with cars. They planned to present me with a new one at the Open. By bringing the car on a transporter it showed how keen they were to emphasize that this was to be a proper presentation. A lot of companies would give a chap a car, let him drive around in it and at some time or another arrange the presentation. There might be 3451 miles on the clock by that time. But BCA wanted it to read zero. They did things professionally.

It didn't take me too long to get back to the job at hand. I spent 30 minutes on the practice ground and 30 minutes on the putting green. During that time I also checked my equipment.

I had put in a four-wood instead of a two-iron. This was a particularly strong four-wood and I felt that I was striking it well. And in practice I had worked out that it was likely that I would need the four-wood more often than a two-iron. Of course, you can never tell because the weather conditions can change so much at St Andrews that holes which are a driver and a wedge one day can become a driver and a long iron or fairway wood the next.

Then it was time to go to the 1st tee. I wished Johnny and Antonio good luck – and we were away. There is very little out of the ordinary to relate about that first round. I finished with 71 which was 3 strokes behind the leader – Isao Aoki of Japan. I can recall that I made a point of using Garrido as a kind of pacemaker. He started off by missing almost every green but he kept chipping the ball dead and saving his score. I thought to myself that if Antonio continued in that fashion he could turn out to be a contender. So I decided I had better keep pace with him. But in the end he finished with 73. And he went on to finish joint twenty-fourth. Johnny also opened with 73, but a second-round 77 led to his missing the 36 hole cut.

Inevitably it was the 17th – the infamous 'Road Hole' – which led to my most heart-breaking moment in the first round. I'm sure every golfer in Britain understands the problems of this soul-searching hole. If they didn't before the 1978 Open, they should certainly now be fully aware of the difficulties. For this Open, the Championship Committee elected to make life even tougher by positioning the tee tight to the fence where the old railway line ran. They had also allowed the rough, to the left of the fairway, to grow. It meant that the drive was semi-blind with danger lurking on both sides. To the right, where the hotel stands and where once the railway sheds spread out, it is out of bounds. But to take the easy route and aim left could leave you a terrible lie in the rough.

Even when you have negotiated the drive, the Road Hole is still ready to bite you. The green is 45 yards long, but in the wrong direction. It faces you like a true enemy so that it can parry your every advance. The pin is usually positioned somewhere around the top shelf of the green where the putting surface is narrowest. If you go over the green, the ball can finish on a macadam road or against the wall. It can also, of course, bounce on the road and over the wall. To drop the ball short of the green is also courting disaster because the Road Bunker is small but very deep. It can require a very delicate shot to escape and settle the ball on the green without it rolling straight over on to the road itself.

For Tsuneyuki Nakajima, one of Japan's best players, the Road Hole and the Road Bunker will remain embedded in his mind as the place which may have cost for him the Open of 1978. In fact some say that Nakajima would have won but for his 'happening' at the 17th in the third round.

Nakajima had opened with rounds of 70 and 71 to be right in contention. In the third round he needed to close with two pars and he would have ended the day just 1 shot off the pace. He was playing with such solidarity that once he had successfully struck his drive at the 17th it seemed that only the next shot could destroy his round. And when he landed it on the green there was a school of thought that he might very well finish 4–3 and share the lead. Then . . . disaster! Nakajima's putt headed for the hole, but now the contours of this remarkable green reached out to snatch the ball. Like a cork being sucked from a river by a swirling eddy, Nakajima's ball changed direction and dropped into the dreaded Road Bunker. It was like being drowned. Now he stood there, in the bunker, peering out, a desolate figure frowning at his misfortune. The crowd, on the other side, could see only his head. They could see a swinging club. I don't know whether they actually realized how many times poor Nakajima attempted to splash out of that bunker. But in the end he needed four attempts. He signed for a 9. And he signed his way out of the 1978 Open.

I felt for him. For I knew in the first round that I had been faced with a similar putt. I had successfully reached the green in 2, but now I needed to aim the putt close to the bunker in order to get the ball near the hole. I made it to 4 feet – but missed the second and took 5. But should anybody think I am making this putt out to be more devilish than it is, let them also ask Brian Barnes. He was 3 under par when he got to the Road Hole and at last it seemed this mighty player was going to present a challenge for golf's most famous title. He, too, reached the green with his second. But, like Nakajima, he putted straight into the bunker. He got out quicker but it still led to a 6. Like me, he finished with 71, but I believe that hole could have disturbed Brian's concentration to such an extent that it weakened his challenge for the title.

The second day should have belonged to Nick Faldo. Well, that's the way I look at it. Once again the weather was fair, slightly grey in the morning but becoming brighter as the day grew older, and I felt good. I was feeling even better after 9 holes because I went out like a train in a 4 under par 32. And there it was, in black and white, Nick Faldo was sharing the lead. It was a moment to treasure, but I had no time to savour the experience. I knew I had to forget the leader board. I had 9 more holes to play.

Those 9 holes took 40 strokes. Some people reckon I choked. Others believe the gathering strength of the wind from the east upset the rhythm of my swing. I admit that I was a little deflated after 3 putting the 13th green, but the lucky breaks didn't come my way. What happened at the monster 14th is a fair illustration of how things didn't work out for me on that back 9.

The 14th is the hole where the Beardies, a group of four bunkers, wait for the errant drive, and Hell Bunker, farther on, provides the severest obstacle for those who try to reach the green in 2. Look for a safe route on the left and inevitably your ball will be gobbled up by either Grave Bunker or the Ginger Beer Bunkers. After 3 putting the 13th, I was keen to strike back. The 14th hardly presented the easiest of holes to do that, but I played the first two shots competently and I left myself a wedge to the green. From the moment I struck it I thought, 'That's it. I'll be putting from close range for a birdie.' I saw it as my chance to fight back to the top of the leader board. Eagerly I waited for the ball to drop and run on. It landed just on the top of a ridge and it should have been inch-perfect. But the ball stopped dead. It didn't move a fraction. I couldn't believe it. The birdie chance had gone and instead it was another bogey.

I kicked myself at that. Just as poor Seve, 7 under par standing on the 17th tee, and Arnold Palmer, must have kicked themselves for driving out of bounds at the unrelenting Road Hole. For both it meant 6s, and Seve, who seemed set to lead on his own, had to share the head of the leader-board at the halfway stage with Aoki and Ben Crenshaw. They were on 139 – 5 under par – and I was 4 behind on 143.

The third round put me right back in the running. I produced my best round of the week – a 70 – and on this occasion the 17th failed to punish me for a wayward second. In fact I got out of jail with one of the most remarkable shots of my life. I had struck my second to the left. Now I had Road Bunker between me and the green. There seemed only one option open to me – to aim to the left and leave myself a longish but uphill putt to try to save the 4. I pondered the shot. I couldn't try a pitch to the pin because the ball would never stop and it would be on the Road. Then John Moorhouse, my caddie, said, 'Go on, just chop it up that bank.' I said that there was absolutely no way I could attempt that. If I did, I ran the danger of sending it straight into the bunker. And I didn't want to be in there.

Nevertheless, it is what I decided to do. I'm not sure whether it was out of sheer bravado or whether I suddenly realized that come the end of the Open a 4 now might be good enough to win and 5 might not. So I hit the ball firmly at the hole. Then it happened. The ball kicked straight right. I put my hands over my eyes. I was seeing sixes and sevens and eights and Nakajimas! Then the crowd began to buzz with excitement. The ball had gone up the face of the green and across the top of the bunker. But no, it was slowly rolling . . . rolling towards the hole. I watched almost with disbelief as it gradually made its way to within 2 feet of the hole. Then I made the putt.

I've watched that shot time and time again on television replays. It looks as if it was the natural thing to do and that the execution of the shot was perfect. I suppose it was, but in real life it was a heart-pounding moment. And that wasn't the last of my worries. At the final hole I struck my drive ever so well, but the ball finished on the road which crosses the monster double fairway of the 1st and 18th. But I clipped the second to 8 feet and I rapped home the putt. I had made two of the best up and downs of my life at the last 2 holes of the home of golf. I felt marvellous.

It also meant that I went into the fourth and final round with an aggregate of 213 – level with three Americans, Tom Kite, Tom Weiskopf and John Schroeder. Only Peter Oosterhuis and Tom Watson, on 211, and Jack Nicklaus, Simon Owen, Isao Aoki and Ben Crenshaw, on 212, were ahead of me. Only 3 strokes separated the leading twelve. We all had a chance of winning the Open and I was determined to give my level best.

At eight o'clock the next morning I woke with chronic chest pains and I was haunted by the fear that I might not even be able to play. I was due out in a little more than four hours with John Schroeder. What was I to do? My mother suggested that perhaps a warm bath would help. Mums always seem to get it right when you're in trouble and this occasion was no exception. I spent half an hour just soaking in the bath and when I stepped out I felt 100 per cent. What had caused the pains is a mystery. Now I was ready for action.

The send-off we received going down the 1st hole was un-believable. The crowd seemed to applaud us all the way. I can remember thinking to myself, 'Gee, this is going to be a hell of a day.' I must admit my stomach felt a little tight. When I'm confident in myself that I'm playing well I don't get nervous. But on this occasion there was every reason to be. It was the last round of the Open and here I was poised to follow in Tony Jacklin's footsteps and keep the championship in Britain.

When I reached the turn in a 1 over par 37 I still had a chance. It was an outside chance, but if I could get hot on the back 9 there was every possibility of victory. The 13th, a little over 400 yards in length, can prove a troublesome hole because the second has to be flighted over a ruck of heathery hills. But on this, the last day of the 1978 Open, the wind had turned around 180 degrees. It meant that holes on the way out, like the 2nd, demanded three- and four-irons for the shots into the green, whereas on the first three days we had been using eight- or nine-irons. But it also meant that the 13th, on the way back, was less formidable. I hit a three-wood from the tee and it left me a wedge to the green. The 13th green was really burnt and I knew that I must land the ball on the front of the green and allow it to roll-up. I felt I struck the shot well and that it was coming down nice and softly. But there is a little ridge at the front and the ball caught it and instead of going forward it went straight left. It hit another bank and that killed it stone dead. I was left with a delicate little chip. With the green in the shape it was, that shot was almost impossible to play and the ball kept rolling and rolling and rolling. It went 20 feet past and I 2 putted. A bogey 5 when I had been looking for a birdie 3.

At the end of the day the 2 strokes were not in themselves enough to lose me the Open. But, although I made a birdie at the 14th, I felt that my impetus was rudely interrupted by the unlucky 13th, and after making pars at the last 4 holes I had to settle for 72 and 285. It meant that I was one of only three players – Nicklaus and Tom Kite were the others – not to card one single round over par throughout the week. But Ray Floyd had already finished with a thrilling last-round 68 for 283 and so my dreams of winning the Open had vanished. It was left to Nicklaus and Simon Owen to provide that sensational finish which ended in Jack adding his third Open to an impressive list of 'Majors' which includes five US Masters, four US PGAs and three US Opens. Will there be another like him?

Nicklaus's last round of 69 gave him a winning total of 281. He finished 2 strokes ahead of Owen, Floyd, Crenshaw and Kite. Oosterhuis, my Ryder Cup team-mate, had a super week but a last-round 73 was not quite good enough and he finished next on 284. I finished joint seventh along with my last-round partner John Schroeder, who closed his championship by holing 20 foot putts at the 17th and 18th, and Bob Shearer of Australia and Aoki.

I headed straight home. I was far from depressed. In fact, I was extremely pleased. I felt that I had proved myself capable of winning an Open one day when the opportunity presented itself. I had survived the test of the last day. I had endured that pulsating moment when we walked down the 1st hole. My nerve-centre had flickered, but it had not faltered.

Gerald Micklem had watched me much of the time. And he forecast afterwards, 'He will be the best British golfer since Henry Cotton.' I aimed to prove him right.

10

Ian Connelly

When I knocked in that short putt to beat Tom Watson in the Ryder Cup in 1977 it left me with a moment to treasure. And for one other person, my coach, Ian Connelly, the occasion was as emotional as it was for me. To him the memory of a big, raw youngster with a half-set of clubs came flooding back. And now I had run out the winner in that exciting encounter with Watson. It was less than five years ago that he had first met me. We had worked as a team to get success and so now Ian had every right to feel pleased at what had been achieved. I was back from a successful Open where I had stuck to the game plan we had worked on before going to St Andrews. We had concentrated on that slightly cut-down swing, to keep the ball under the wind, and it had worked so well.

At the same time it would be correct to say that technically I was not completely 100 per cent at St Andrews. I never felt that my game was really at its best and so, instead of going on to the next tournament, the Dutch Open, I stayed at home for a restful week. Rest? Hardly that! A visit to Ian a short drive away at Dyrham Park and it was back to fundamentals. Back to making sure that I quickly eliminated any faults creeping into my game.

After ten years at Welwyn Garden City, Ian had moved to Dyrham Park, ten miles away, early in 1976. A native of Dundee and initially a member of the Downfield club, Ian became a very fine amateur player. The late Jack McLean, professional for many years at Gleneagles, was instrumental in getting Ian his first paid post – as assistant to Ian Marchbank at Turnberry. Ian talks about his two years at Turnberry, on the Ayrshire coast, as being very informative and I suppose it is a bit of a coincidence that most of my best performances have come on links courses.

Nevertheless, Ian reckons his enthusiasm for coaching comes from the time he spent with Jimmy Adams at Royal Mid Surrey. Jimmy, one of golf's great enthusiasts and a marvellous player, taught Ian more in twelve months than most people learn in a decade of education. So by the time he arrived at Welwyn Garden City in 1966 he was already gaining a reputation as one of the country's top teaching professionals.

By the time we met, Ian was certainly an established coach, with a number of promising youngsters, most of them Herts Colts players, regularly visiting him for instruction. So I count myself rather fortunate that Ian quickly took an interest in me and started to coach me after my first few lessons with Chris Arnold. I was desperately keen to learn and succeed. Ian saw the potential in me and he chose to fire my ambition with constant chat about champions and championships, and was always telling me how good I *would* become. He thought it predictable that I would successfully progress from boys' golf, through to youths' and to the England senior team, which I did. That faith inspired me and gave me the confidence to go out and win. He set the goals, higher and tougher every week, and I had to succeed – or suffer the consequences. Ian can read the riot act and so you don't want to make too many mistakes. But I always had one asset on my side . . . I was willing to work and work and work.

In a junior golf column in a magazine Ian wrote about my approach to the game, commenting, 'He listened attentively, asked a lot of questions, and, most of all, spent hour after hour practising the fundamentals that I had been preaching to him. One day after giving Nick a lesson on tempo, I told him, half-seriously, to go and practise it for the rest of the afternoon. Five hours later as I was about to leave for the day, Nick came marching in and informed me that he had "got it". That is the stuff that champions are made of !'

With Ian, it has always been the simple approach. He will point out time and again that there is no such person as a natural golfer. You can be athletically gifted but golf is a sport that you have to learn. To understand it you must have a sound knowledge of the fundamentals and therefore, after returning from St Andrews, it was back to basics to see if there was any part of my game which really required an overhaul.

Sometimes it means going over old ground. But it is never dull. In my view, the reward of listening is reflected in your progress. Back in 1973 both Ken Brown and I were listed in Ian's appointments book as: Ken Brown, age 16, handicap 3. Nick Faldo, age 15, handicap 7. One year later it showed K. Brown, age 17, handicap 3; N. Faldo, age 16, handicap 3. Ken, of course, is now a very fine golfer. But I know that during the one year under Ian's coaching he was more inclined to do his own thing than try out Ian's suggestions. I believe, no matter how good you are at your chosen profession, it makes sense to listen to people and try their advice. If, after a fair test, it does not seem to be contributing to your progress then it can be forgotten. But give it a go.

With Ian, I knew from the start I could rely on him for all kinds of advice. After my superb amateur year in 1975 it was a struggle to decide what to do next because I needed a new incentive. I discussed the whole affair with Ian and, after a lot of discussion, it came down to either turning professional or accepting the golf scholarship at Houston University.

Ian thought Houston was the best idea at the time, because he felt that I needed more competitive experience as an amateur and that there was no better way to obtain that than in the United States. Of course, we know that Houston went wrong. But I would never blame Ian for that. I know he wanted me to stick it out there a bit longer, but when I got back we had a heart-to-heart session and I think he accepted my reasoning that the most important thing to me is that nothing shall occur which is detrimental to my game.

Ian monitors my progress in some ingenious ways. In my early days I would marvel at how solid players like Peter Oosterhuis, Brian Huggett and Jack Newton struck the ball. One day, about a year after I had first seen the top professionals in action, Ian asked how they impressed me now. I replied that I wasn't quite so impressed as I once had been. He winked and said, 'That's great – it means your own game is improving.'

That gave me a bit of a kick, and all the time Ian would cleverly bring up points such as that to illustrate to me that I was beginning to get to grips with the game.

Mind you, there was every reason for my game to get better. I virtually lived in Ian's pro shop at Welwyn Garden City and on the practice range. Even in the winter I would sweep the snow, if necessary, off the driving net so I could keep swinging. I would stand there in the icy cold and hit balls until my hands were too numb to hold the club any longer. Then I would return to the pro shop for a chat with Ian. He might suggest something that I wanted to try out straight away. So I used to nip outside and Ian would watch and I would go back inside and he would tell me if I had got it right. I never left for home until he and I were satisfied.

Initially, Ian taught me the American-style method – very upright. He pointed out that the simplest way to swing a club would be in a circle. But, as we are not built to do it that way, we must do the next best thing. Being a tall person I can do it; I come back a fraction inside, hold it square and bang – straight through to the target. As long as the club-face is square the ball will go where you want it – it's fundamentals that's all. Ian stressed from the start that you must work entirely on getting the grip, address and alignment right.

Rhythm and tempo are also extremely important. Ian told me after I got back from the Open that I owed my high finish – and also my victory in the Colgate earlier in the year – to great tempo and composure. That was another thing he had helped me with when I first took up the game. I was not very good on the mental side. In fact, I used to lose my temper quite a bit. So we had a chat one rainy afternoon and he brought it home to me that if I continued to lose my cool on the course when things went wrong I would never win. He pointed out that, if you are not in command of yourself, you can't expect to keep the game going on the days when you are not swinging at your best. He still criticizes me if he feels that it is necessary. He says he is my biggest fan and my biggest critic. In fact, after my win in the Colgate, he rebuked me over an incident involving the gallery at the 17th. He was proud of the win, but he still made the point that I had been rather brusque with the crowd and that I should be highly conscious at all times of the public relations side of golf. It was another lesson learned.

By staying at home to work on my game with Ian, I missed an unusual incident in the Dutch Open when the word strike found its way into the golfer's vocabularly. The European Tournament Players Division claimed three Americans, not members of the US PGA, were ineligible to compete and called on 120 members to boycott the championship. Only twenty-eight players, mostly Dutch, took part on the first day, and some of the British professionals returned home, but the tournament went ahead twenty-four hours later reduced to 54 holes, with the first round written off. The irony was that victory eventually went to Bob Byman, the defending champion, who was a member of the American group which toured Europe the previous year and created the initial controversy. Byman by then had earned his US PGA card and the Dutch venue for the tournament was Noordwijk – just three miles away from the Noordwyksche course where Ian Connelly spent two years full-time teaching in the early sixties. So we both read about the incident with interest – but I'm glad I remained at home.

I I

Aced by Jacko

After spending a week practising at home, I arrived in Cologne for the German Open 'frightened' by my swing! It is a peculiarity of golf that you can work hard on the fundamentals and when you get to the scene of the event something feels wrong. In the practice round I realized that I was using the top half of my body too much and losing my timing. So it is an understatement to say that I was shaken to learn on reaching the 4th tee on the first day that Seve Ballesteros had already finished with an 8 under par course record of 64!

My concern was tempered by the knowledge that I had saved my par at the 1st with a good 'up and down' and then managed to collect birdies at the 495 yard 2nd and at the 181 yard 3rd. The latter was achieved when a sweet five-iron tee shot finished no more than 6 inches from the hole. That reassured me that I had regained my tempo but I knew I would need to make at least another six birdies to keep pace with Seve. It appeared out of the question.

The Cologne Refrath course, 6750 yards long, is comparable to some to be found in South Africa, and therefore Gary Player, who was making a rare appearance on the Continent, was expected to feel at home. Fifty years previously the land on which we were playing was part of a swamp area, but it had drained sufficiently for a Dr Von Limburger to be asked in 1938 to design a course through the Koenigsforst (King's Forest). It was not, however, until 1955 that the full 18 holes, which meander through the forest, were eventually opened. The Second World War delayed construction and there were financial difficulties before the course could be completed. In 1957 the German Open, first played in Baden-Baden in 1911,

Jack Nicklaus, who inspired me to take up the game, gives his caddie a hug after winning the 1978 Open at St Andrews.

Ken Brown, a Hertfordshire Colts colleague and now a fellow professional on the European tour.

Severiano Ballesteros, basking in the glory of his 1979 Open win, never stops smiling as he talks to the world's press.

Peter Oosterhuis lines up a putt as we move towards victory against Jack Nicklaus and Ray Floyd in the 1977 Ryder Cup.

everiano Ballesteros powerfully strikes another shot on the way to his istoric win in the 1979 Open.

John Jacobs, one of golf's leading instructors and captain of the 1979
European Ryder Cup team.

was taken to Cologne and it was then that Harry Weetman, the late and respected Ryder Cup player and captain, compiled the course record of 66 which had stood firm until Seve's stunning 64.

That brilliant start helped to soothe some of the discontent of fans and sponsors Braun, who were upset that Arnold Palmer, whose appearance had been widely publicized, was not playing because he could not secure a release from the Greater Hartford Open, a conflicting tournament in America. In order to protect their tours, the governing bodies have a strict code of conduct with regard to conflicting events. For instance, in order to contribute towards the success of the European Tournament Players Division tournaments, the leading twenty-five players in the current year and the previous year, if residents of Europe, or members of the current Ryder Cup or Hennessy Cup teams, generally speaking are not permitted to compete in any tournament or exhibition match, private or public, scheduled against a major ETPD event, unless written permission is obtained from the secretary of the ETPD. Clearly the sponsors of the tournament that particular week are also consulted. The rules are similar on both sides of the Atlantic and extended to cover 'overseas' players. Because he felt so upset by the entire affair, Palmer informed Herwig Zahm, president of Braun International, that he would personally reimburse any United States serviceman who came especially to see him play that week. Even though the great Arnold Palmer was missed, I am sure none of the spectators left the course on that opening day disappointed.

As Seve, who set the pattern for his round with an eagle at his second hole followed by three birdies, sat down for lunch in the clubhouse, I was making my own challenge. I'm willing to admit that initially I entertained no thoughts of equalling Seve's supreme achievement. The only target I set myself was to get close enough so as not to lose touch with him after only one round. Seve, in the mood, can reduce a tournament to a race for the runners-up spot.

So I went to work to erode Seve's advantage. The putter was doing me a few favours and I popped in nice ones of 12 feet and 8 feet at the 6th and 8th holes respectively to reach the turn in 32. That spurred me on and provided me with a tonic because I was on a course of pills for swollen glands and was in a certain amount of discomfort. There could be no better medicine than a few more birdies on the back 9, but they were slow in coming, or else I might have stunned even myself and swept ahead. I reached the 14th tee still 4 under par – and 4 behind Seve.

Then I warmed to the task. I holed good putts for birdies at the 14th and 15th and, pumped-up and ready to accept anything, I tram-lined a 40-footer across the green and into the cup for another at the 17th. I was left needing an eagle 3 at the long 18th to take the lead. Seve was now almost certainly back at his hotel, relaxing with the thought that surely a 64 would give him a comfortable lead, and I began to wonder how he would greet the news if I could finish with 63. That prospect perished when I missed the green on the right-hand side with my approach. But I was still determined to equal his 64 and, after chipping to 8 feet, I gave the putt a good chance and joyfully watched as the ball rolled into the cup.

It was my best round since turning professional and I felt that it could hardly have come at a sweeter moment. The victory in the Colgate and my high finish in the Open, for which I received £3937, had helped lift me to the head of the Order of Merit. I now had £19,855 and Seve, who had been the leader for the last two seasons, was trailing me by £3684. So I was anxious not to allow him to overhaul me. Seve had already suggested to the press that 'It's going to be tough overtaking Nick' but he had also issued a challenge by stressing, 'I've got to do it because I want to be top after the Carrolls Irish Open at the end of next month [August].'

I felt it was I who now held a psychological advantage as far as the German Open was concerned. But there was a long way to go with colleague John Morgan, South African John Fourie and Rhodesian Simon Hobday all grouped together on 66 and Player only one stroke further back in a group on 67.

On the second day, I performed as well as I did during the opening round, but finished nine strokes worse. From tee to green my game was solid, but the critical factor was that the putts didn't drop. I stroked the ball with the same kind of authority on the greens, but there are days when your luck deserts you and this just happened to be one of them. I finished

with 73 for 137 while Seve firmly established his claim to the
first prize by collecting three birdies in his last 4 holes. It gave
him 67 for a 13 under par total of 131. In spite of that
marvellous halfway score he still insisted he was unhappy with
his game!

Gary Player, marvelling at the driver and three-iron which
Seve used to reach the 528 yard 18th, had another viewpoint.
'After seeing that, thank goodness I've won my tournaments
already,' he said. 'This man is changing the face of golf.' I
thought to myself that I would be trying my best to change it
with him. However, my hopes of winning the German Open
had been dampened and over the last two days my game went
a little off the boil. Seve stayed out in front, although he was
given a bit of a fright when that consistent competitor Neil
Coles came through with a last-round 65. In the end Seve
finished with 67 for 168 – 2 ahead of Coles and 3 in front of
South African John Bland. I finished 11th.

The disappointment of falling out of contention was increased by the knowledge that Seve now went to the top of
the Order of Merit. He had won £6095 compared to my £5560
and, although none of us realized at the time, it began for him
an astonishing spell. In five successive appearances he won
three Continental Opens – German, Scandinavian and Swiss –
and on the other two occasions he finished only one shot behind
the winners. It transformed the season for him, for until arriving in Germany, he had managed only one win on the European
circuit – in the Martini International. Of course, it should not
be forgotten that, before the curtain had gone up on the 1978
European circuit, Seve had staggered the Americans by winning
the Greater Greensboro Open – one week before the US
Masters in which he also competed.

For me, the German Open was a bittersweet affair for
another reason. An extra prize at stake was a £17,000
Mercedes 450 SL for the first professional to hole in one. And
on my first day in Germany, at the first short hole I played,
I had my partners slapping me on the back as my six-iron tee
shot went straight into the cup. There was only one snag –
my partners were amateurs because we were playing in a pro-
am and that gleaming motor-car was not on offer until the
tournament itself began one day later.

I felt a little despondent that evening. Instead of flying home to Britain at the end of the week, I could have jumped into the car and driven back in style. Actually, in that first round of 64 the next day, I again came so close to winning the car when my tee shot at the same hole – this time with a five-iron – made it to within half an inch of the cup, but on this occasion stayed out.

In the evening I had dinner with Tony Jacklin and I suppose I was talking quite a bit about my misfortune. Tony, in jest, said that he could make me feel even worse by holing in one tomorrow. So we had a little wager that if either one of us made an ace we would give the other £1000.

You cannot imagine how stunned I was when on the third day the news filtered through to me that Tony had done just that – holed his six-iron tee shot at the 182 yard 15th! At first I couldn't believe it. Then I couldn't wait to see Tony – and he certainly wasn't hard to spot as photographers gathered round to catch him gleefully sitting at the wheel of the Mercedes. He gave me a wink and a smile – and I knew that I had earned the easiest 'grand' of my life. It was some slight compensation for not winning that Mercedes, I suppose, but a hole-in-one jinx stayed with me throughout 1978.

I'm sure that the most enjoyable ace any golfer can experience is the first one. I believe that is because it is a shot which you think will never happen to you. So when I holed out at the 3rd at Welwyn Garden City on 14 May 1973 I went crazy. The thrill of watching the ball dive into the cup is staggering and I was leaping all over the course shouting, 'I've holed it! I've holed it!' A couple of weeks before the German Open I had narrowly missed another ace at WGC when there was nothing less at stake than . . . a Rolls-Royce!

It was during my pre-Open head-to-head encounter with Gary Player. The Rolls had been put up only for an ace at the 18th hole to provide an exciting climax to our match. So the day before, I went down to the club and practised the shot. I decided that I had to stretch myself with a four-iron and hit the ball at the middle of the green with a gentle fade. In practice, I got to within 2 feet and I felt confident that I could get it close when the time came in the match. Well, I could not have got it closer than I did. Gary and the crowd watched in astonishment as the ball bounced, gripped and then, on the second bounce, hit the back of the hole. We all thought it was going to go in, but, as luck would have it, the ball stayed out. I think the car was worth in the region of £40,000. So I was probably half an inch away from the biggest prize of my life.

Yet the hole-in-one saga did not end with Welwyn Garden City and Cologne. It continued later in the year when I grabbed an ace in the third round of the European Open at Walton Heath. At the time it was an important shot in terms of challenging for that championship because I had been losing ground. But the thought did cross my mind when the ball went in the hole that there might be a special prize. I hurried back to find John Simpson, who looks after my affairs in Mark McCormack's International Management Group, to see if he had found out if there was anything in the programme. But there was nothing. I didn't even receive a bottle of champagne. A few days later we found out that the organizers of the European Open had contemplated putting up a Jaguar XJS for an ace. They decided against that idea, but then considered the possibility of a £10,000 cash jackpot. In the end they didn't bother with anything.

So you can understand how I feel about holes-in-one! My biggest prize is still for my first ace at Welwyn Garden City when the club presented me with . . . a hole-in-one tie!

12
The 'Walking One-Iron'

Seve Ballesteros's win in Germany had piled pressure on me. There was a passport to the World Series of Golf in America for the leader of the European Order of Merit at the end of August. Now, as we went into that very month, Seve had nipped ahead of me. I had £1750 to make up and I knew it was going to be a tough fight. The Scandinavian Enterprise Open, over the Vasatorps course near Helsingborg in Sweden, was the scene of the next confrontation. But by the time the first two rounds were over, I knew that Seve had the initiative. He opened with rounds of 73 and 69. I began with 75 and 77. I was 10 shots worse off.

In fact, nobody really knew how we were all placed in the event because heavy rain and lightning on the second day led to a crazy situation which left some of the players with 36 hole scores and others needing to go out the next day and complete their second round before playing the third. For me the second round was ridiculous for another reason. I struck only three poor shots, but one finished unplayable in rocks, another went into water and the third found its way into a rotten lie. People find it strange that after carding a 77 you can say that you played well. But I reckon I did.

On the third day, I was determined to prove that my game was in good shape. I had given myself a sharp talking to at the start of the season with regard to never throwing the towel in : I made myself a promise that, whatever the situation, I would fight my way as high as possible in the final list of all tournaments. In the end, I fired final rounds of 67 and 69. What a difference that made. I had played the first 36 holes in 8 over par and the last 36 in 8 under. I moved through the field and finished in joint sixteenth position.

I rated that one of my best performances of the season. It showed that I could fight my way back. But there was no stopping Seve and he completed the week with 68 and 69 to edge out Dale Hayes by one stroke. The £6944 he earned took Seve clear at the head of the Order of Merit. He was beginning to pull away and, although Dale had hung on well, both he and I knew that it was going to take somebody special to halt Seve's winning run.

That somebody special turned out to be Lee Trevino. Yet, in a way, both Seve and I combined to give Lee the next title on the European tour – the Benson and Hedges International Open at Fulford, near York. Circumstances, rather than ability, can often dictate your game and I believe, from my own point of view, there is no better example than the Benson and Hedges. My early season thunder and Seve's revival had made the pair of us exciting news for the golf writers. Our head-to-head confrontation was all the rage.

So, after Mark James had set the early pace, it was Seve and I who stirred the golfing world in the third round. First Seve appeared to be heading for a supporting role in the tournament when he began his third day by 3 putting the 1st and 5th holes. He was then seven shots behind pace-setting Mark. It seemed that Seve's hopes of collecting a record third successive win had disappeared. Yet he now turned on his golfing magic by carding six birdies and one eagle in his last 11 holes. It led to an inward 9 of 30, giving him a round of 65 and a total of 205.

Both James and Tienie Britz, one of the large contingent of South African players who compete regularly in Europe, did enough to tie Seve on 205. I was out ninety minutes after Seve and, although I saw his name rise on the leader board, I must admit that at the time I did not realize he was making such a forceful move. I just went my own way and compiled a 66 which enabled me to finish on 204 and lead the field. I didn't play the back 9 too smartly, but nevertheless the door had now swung open on the prospect of my second big win of 1978.

I felt that the last day was going to be a great one for me. It was an advantage to be paired with Seve, because it gave me the opportunity to keep my eyes on what he was doing. Ironically, that was to contribute to my downfall. For at the 2nd hole I made a stupid mistake – one that I regretted afterwards. Seve struck a great shot into the 2nd green and he was clearly going to turn it into a birdie. I was 30 feet from the hole and the only thing in my mind when I stood over the putt was to hole it in order that Seve didn't get an early break. My keenness to make the putt led to the ball running 4 feet past the hole and I missed it on the way back. Seve made a mess of the 4th and, if I had not tried to be so clever at the second, I would have retained my advantage.

For those first few holes, there can be no doubt that I played Seve and not the tournament. I think that Seve was also thinking more about my score than about what the other challengers were doing. So both Trevino and Neil Coles used their experience to move steadily through the field. Lee was helped by a truly amazing shot at the 4th where he struck a one-iron approach from 206 yards and saw the ball strike the pin and dive into the cup for a most extraordinary eagle 2. But there was certainly nothing lucky about the 66 that he brilliantly composed to set a 10 under par target of 274. It is probably fair to say that both Seve and I would have beaten that score if we had not been so concerned with watching each other during the start of the final round. Instead, we both finished 1 shot behind and it was Neil Coles and Noel Ratcliffe, an Australian, who finished tied with Trevino.

Noel only lasted 1 hole in the sudden-death play-off. But Lee and Neil went 4 holes before the title was decided. Neil eventually drove into trees and Lee came home the winner. I was left to reflect on my second shot to the 18th which looked certain to follow the pattern of the majority of approaches to that green and run up close to the flag. Instead, it stopped dead and my chance disappeared. But I learned a vital lesson. I knew that in future the presence of Seve, or for that matter any other challenger, would not divert my attention from playing my own game.

There are few more insular golfers than Ken Brown. We kind of grew up together, golfing-wise, since we played in the same Herts Colts team in which I cannot recall us being beaten as a pair. Ken has always had a willowy build and I think it was at the Benson and Hedges that Lee christened him 'the walking one-iron'. It was also at the Benson and Hedges that Ken revealed he was running into form when he reeled off a superb final round of 63. He had been too far back to trouble the leaders, but it was a sure sign that he was going to be a challenger for the Carrolls Irish Open at Portmarnock the following week.

Because of his slender frame – Ken is 6 feet tall but he weighs in at around 10 stone – it might be thought that he cannot strike the ball as far as most of the pros on the tour. Don't you believe it! When we were youngsters it is a fact that Ken relied heavily upon his short game. He needed two full-blooded woods to get up at some par 4s and, since he was striking 200 yard shots to the green a lot of the time, it must be obvious that he missed putting surfaces fairly frequently. So Ken had to make sure that he had a sharper short game than his rivals. But since those days Ken has put yards and yards on his driving and he now hits it as far as most.

Therefore, the 7097 yard Portmarnock circuit was no longer a problem to him in terms of length when the 1978 Carrolls began on 24 August. Indeed with his sound short game it is the type of track which is tailor-made for a player such as Ken. For when the battle is on it is not hard to miss the Portmarnock greens on the back 9 and then it comes down to a question of how many times you can get up and down. In the end that is exactly what happened in Ireland.

I like playing at Portmarnock. The first 3 holes, all of them a little under 400 yards long, are a bit cramped, but then the course spreads its wings. It certainly must be one of the finest genuine links courses in the world. For the spectator it can be most rewarding for the course is built on a peninsula of links-land, which lies between the Irish Sea and an inland bay. So there can be great views and great golf.

Unfortunately, the best golf at the start of the Carrolls didn't come from me. Defending champion Hubert Green, who was leading a strong contingent of American challengers including Tom Weiskopf, Bill Rogers and Lanny Wadkins, went off in a rush with a glorious opening round of 67. I had played one of my Open Championship practice rounds at St Andrews with Hubert and on his day he can be a masterful player. He has a unique putting action, crouching extremely low for such a tall man, and it was no surprise for me to come in following a first round of 73 to find Hubert leading.

However, Hubert's hopes of a second successive Irish Open win crashed when he took 76 in the second round. I didn't fare much better and a second 73 put me 7 strokes behind the new leader – Ireland's own John O'Leary – and at the end of the third round they were still cheering because he had stayed in front. But both Tom Weiskopf and Green, who shot 67 and 69 respectively, had ominously moved into the picture and Brown's 70 to O'Leary's 71 took him within a stroke of the leader.

Germany's Bernhard Langer also began the fourth and final round trailing by the minimum margin and he had a special reason for wanting to win – it was his 21st birthday! For a while it seemed likely that the champagne corks would be popping for Bernhard, but he eventually faded away.

For much of the week it seemed that Seve was unlikely to make the news . . . for once! Everything was all quiet on the Spanish front and his utter domination of European golf through the month of August seemed to be at an end. He had opened with rounds of 71, 72 and 74. That left him 7 strokes off the pace and before he set out on the final day he claimed that he needed eight birdies to stand a chance. If that was the case I needed about ten or eleven! For a third-round 74 had failed to improve my position. In the end, I put together a final round of 69 which was even better than the score suggests. But it was still only good enough for joint eighteenth.

Seve? Well, he did it again. Not just eight birdies – he got nine instead! It gave him a course record of 65 and he had set the pace in the clubhouse with a 6 under par total of 282. Since Seve had set out some two hours before the leaders, it must have been unnerving to O'Leary and Brown to see the name of Ballesteros on the leader board at 6 under par with 72 holes played. And suddenly it was a wide open race as the Americans Green and Weiskopf breathed fire into their games and launched eleventh-hour challenges.

Weiskopf apparently played super golf, but his putter let him down. Green, however, came to the last hole needing a birdie to edge ahead of Seve. It is the kind of situation in which you must attack but Hubert's determined effort to retain his title folded when he was bunkered twice at the 18th. So it came down to Brown and O'Leary. Both had started the event as 50–1 outsiders; now a huge section of the 60,000 people who watched the Carrolls that week were stretching to get a glimpse as both strode up the 18th. Somewhere Seve was also living in hope that he might still win the title. If both Brown and O'Leary dropped a shot each it would be a three-way sudden-death play-off. And for a long time that seemed a distinct possibility.

Brown drove into rough. O'Leary into sand. Brown shanked his second into the stands on the right; O'Leary made a fine recovery, but he was still short of the green in two. The crowd were beginning to look for the quickest route to the first extra hole. The TV producer was seeking to capture the drama at the 18th but his brain was working overtime as he began to realize that the end might now not come on this green but somewhere further out in the country. Pat Heneghan, the Carrolls Tournament Director had everything ready for the presentation, but at the same time he was probably crossing his fingers that it went to 'extra-time'. It would be a classic play-off for Ireland, with O'Leary battling against Ballesteros, the King of Europe, and Brown.

It still seemed on when Brown, allowed a free drop in a dropping zone exactly 77 yards from the hole, pitched the ball to 12 feet. If you were a betting man the money would now be on O'Leary but his pitch was too delicate and he left the ball outside Brown's. The partisan crowd began to feel that fate was against their hero. They hushed for O'Leary's putt from 16 feet. But it missed and now Brown had a 12-footer for his first big title. I think that by now the crowd had accepted that Brown was certain to slot it home. He had underlined his superb short game by single-putting 5 of the last 6 holes. So this was just another putt of the length which seems easy for him. Of course, the pressure was on, but it didn't seem to bother our Ken. He carefully lined up the putt and the ball went straight into the cup.

It made me think back to our days together in the Herts Colts team. For there never seemed any doubt when Ken was younger that the putts wouldn't drop for him. But there was one thing different in those days – Ken had a reputation of being 'Joe Lightning'. He would walk up to a putt and strike it almost immediately. He walked the fairways fast and struck the shots with machine-gun rapidity. Yet, after that Irish Open win Ken seemed to get in the headlines more for his slow play than his game. I don't know why he has allowed himself to become so slow, for it is relatively simple to develop a routine which ensures that you go at a fair speed. In my opinion, Ken doesn't have such a routine and therefore he would probably do himself a favour if he worked towards getting one. Let's face it, if you are a 'club thrower' you work hard to erase that element from your game. It destroys you – and other golfers. Ken's got a reputation for being slow; if he can't change, it is a poor show.

Then again, he has always rebelled. He always wanted to do his own thing. He had lessons with Ian Connelly but after being shown something or other he would simply try it for ten minutes. He never persevered. He never seemed prepared to listen to good advice long enough for it to do him any good.

The following week the tour moved to Switzerland. There can be few more spectacular settings for golf events than the switchback Alpine course at Crans-sur-Sierre. It is set 5000 feet above the Rhône Valley, ringed by snow-capped peaks. In the winter it is a skiing resort and it is only for four or five months of the year that golf can be played. I find it strange that the Swiss Open is not staged nearer to a city like Geneva. It is a long trek to reach Crans and the course is not a fair test. In 1978, I was feeling happy after rounds one and two. It had come back to the old dogfight. Seve had opened with a couple of 68s and I had matched them. That was pretty fair scoring because we had endured two freezing cold days – snow even fell on the first! Yet it was nothing compared with the achievement of Jose-Maria Canizares, my Spanish partner for the third round. I began to fall back after driving behind a tree at the first and running up a 7. But Jose began to chase compatriot Seve.

Jose had closed his second round with five birdies. Now, to my utter amazement he began the third round with six success-ive birdies. Then he drove the 317 yard 7th – the ball flies much further in the rarefied air of Alp country – and holed from 18 feet for an eagle. He lipped out for a 2 at the next, but birdied the 9th for outward figures of 4-3-2 3-3-3 2-3-4 = 27. It was a European record – beating the 28s of Bernard Hunt, Peter Mills and John Panton. At that time Andy North and Mike Souchak were the only two Americans to have produced 27s.

For a while, it seemed I might see the 60 barrier broken. But the magic left Jose and he had to settle for 64. It still gave him a 2 stroke edge on Ballesteros, but Seve eased his way in front again in the last round and a fourth successive 68 gave him the Swiss Open for a second successive season. It also gave him a third win in five weeks. It gave him European record winnings of £46,450. And it surely left Hale Irwin, who shared third place with Canizares and Bob Charles behind runner-up Manuel Pinero, returning home to America to confirm that Europe had in Ballesteros a player of immense ability.

13
Seve and Me

In the month of September 1978 I had three confrontations with Seve – but only two of them took place on golf courses. Our first meeting needed a referee and Seve and I had a lot of things to say about each other. In fact, I revealed to the 'ref' that we were good friends off the course – but thumped each other in private! Of course, it was a bit of a joke. For, quite seriously, the rivalry that developed between us was good for our games. Seve's achievements had set targets at which I could aim; and, with me pushing him, it was inevitable that he would go on producing better golf.

The 'referee' during our discussion was Renton Laidlaw of the London *Evening Standard*. He had brought us together for a face-to-face chat for the readers of *Golf World* magazine. We talked about numerous things, but America was high on the list, since at that time Seve had secured the top spot in the European Order of Merit for a third successive year and the possibility of his crossing the Atlantic was a big topic of conversation. Seve said that he couldn't ever see himself playing full-time in America and, of course, he elected to remain in Europe the following season. My own view is that playing in the States might be a little restrictive and I think I would prefer to be a world-wide golfing star, a little like Graham Marsh, the Australian. They call him the golfing globetrotter. He has played and won in America, but he has also established a tremendous reputation in the Far East and in Japan where he has won countless events.

Graham is an extremely consistent player and one thing that Seve and I talked about for some time was the fact that both of us were seeking greater consistency in our games. Seve pointed

94

out that he was changing his game from attack-attack-attack to containing himself a little better so that he was not quite so impetuous. Anybody who witnessed his Open Championship win less than one year later would have doubted those words, but nevertheless there were signs during the next twelve months that Seve was prepared to play conservatively when necessary.

That may, of course, have stemmed from a growing concern over his back problem. We spoke about practising to make ourselves more consistent and Seve pointed out that he could only do about one hour a day for fear of aggravating his back. It contrasted sharply with my own routine which was, and still is, to put in an average of four hours a day. I think it surprises a great number of people that golf is not just a case of driving up to the clubhouse, changing and going on to the course. For me it is about spending hour after hour on the putting green. Hour after hour on the practice range. Yet I get a kick out of practising. You can make it more interesting by setting yourself tests of ability. At home I like to chip out of a bunker over some bushes and into a bucket. Why not try it for yourself – it might take 2 or 3 shots off your handicap !

Seve and I shook hands and went our separate ways after our unique face-to-face had finished . . . but it wasn't long before we were going head-to-head again. This time we were back in Belgium for the Laurent Perrier International and as this tournament finished, the article about Seve and me appeared on the bookstalls. It was quite a coincidence, as it followed another confrontation between us.

The Laurent Perrier was being talked about as a 'rubber match'. Seve had won the inaugural event in 1976 and I had taken the title the next year. The Royal Waterloo course is also an ideal sight for a battle royal and it has nothing to do with playing on the ground where Wellington and Napoleon's men faced each other in 1815. It is simply that the course has been fashioned in such a way that everything can change on the closing stretch. There are relatively few trouble spots on the opening 9 holes, but shortly after the turn the course meanders through a thick wood and if you are not careful your score can get away from you. But emerge intact from this stretch and you go out into the open again for 3 closing par

5s, where an ordinary 70 can be turned into a 66 or a 67.

Seve and I soon proved that to be the case. He grabbed a birdie and an eagle in the closing stretch for a 67 and a couple of birdies kept me in touch with 69. On the middle day – the Laurent Perrier is a 54 hole event – Gene Littler, the American golfer with tremendous tempo and a classic swing, gave another indication of how Royal Waterloo can succumb when he birdied the last four holes. Seve's 72 kept him in front on 139 but now Littler was second on 140. I was 1 stroke further back after a 72.

There can be no doubt that the third and final round gripped the spectators in a way that one could never have conceived following the outward 9. I had prayed for wind, for I thought the only way I could catch and overtake Seve on the last day was for a stiff breeze to blow. I reckoned that he had one suspect shot at that time. When the wind blows you need to punch your shots a bit more and it struck me that Seve was suspect when he tried to play that kind of stroke. When we got to the first tee with a gale blowing I was warmed by the knowledge that I had the right conditions to engineer the execution of Seve in the shadow of the Battle of Waterloo.

Some execution! Seve, bunkered at the 1st for a bogey, then whistled off five birdies and before I knew where I was he had gone 7 strokes ahead of me. With only 11 holes to play it would not have surprised me if the spectators had all disappeared to start celebrating Seve's success with a glass (or two) of the sponsor's champagne. I must admit that mentally I was also beginning to settle for second place, but at the 8th and 9th I managed a couple of birdies and Seve made an error at the 9th which confirmed my opinion of his game being unsettled by the wind. We had been hitting wedges for our second shots to this hole on the first and second days, but now it required a two-iron. Seve tried to punch it in nice and low but he just came over on it and the ball finished left of the green. Nevertheless it still gave him a chance to show us all what a unique character he is. There was a bunker between him and the flag and it was impossible for him to play a pitch shot and get the ball close. So he took out his putter and gave the ball a good whack – hoping to run it through the sand and up on to the green! It almost worked. The ball seemed to be coming out but at the last moment it ran out of momentum and fell back into the bunker. So Seve dropped a shot and my 20 foot downhill putt for a birdie left me only 4 behind. Now there was something to work on.

The 11th momentarily flattened me. Seve walked up to a 20 foot putt, gave it no more than a glance and rolled it straight into the cup for a birdie. He almost seemed to be sprinting. It is in this situation that the pace of another player can often destroy your own game. But even though I was 5 behind I refused to be intimidated. Seve's wayward second to the 9th had given me hope that he might make further errors during the wooded stretch of the course. And I knew that if he dropped a couple of strokes at one hole it would put some doubt into his mind. So I stayed calm and birdies at the 13th and 15th reduced my deficit to 3.

Then came the moment when everything changed. Seve cut his tee shot deep into the trees on the right at the long 16th and he was in trouble. A birdie at that hole would have probably secured the title for him. Instead he took 6 and I made the birdie, a good one straight into the wind, and now the difference was 2. There was incredible drama at the 17th. He struck a good drive down the middle but I hit mine into rough on the left. The ball finished in what I thought was a tractor rut but I couldn't get relief and so I had to play it as best as I could. I managed to hack it 100 yards forward but it seemed that Seve held command again. But his five-iron approach dropped straight into a bunker. It gave me an opening but I had to hit a wedge shot downwind and the ball travelled through to the back of the green. Seve splashed out to 8 feet and I rolled my putt 6 feet past. Now he had another chance to put the matter beyond doubt. But he missed and I realized if I made mine I could win. The putt dropped and we walked to the 18th with only a stroke separating us.

I slammed two drivers to be pin high to the green on the right. He was down at the bottom of a slope from where he faced a tough pitch and he only got it to 12 feet. I pitched to 4 feet. He missed. I holed – and we were level. I had made up 7 strokes in 11 holes. It was freaky. Some people reckon that it was the fact that I was chasing Seve which inspired my counter-attack. But I can't go along with that. It became a challenge to catch the leader, and whether it was Seve or any one of the other competitors in the eight-man field made no difference.

But I still had to win the title. At the first extra hole we both scored regulation pars. At the 2nd, a shortish par 4, he walloped his drive close to the green, but his pitch, obstructed by a fir tree, was too strong. Mine was good, 6 feet away, and I made it for the £4500 top cheque. The money didn't matter too much. What was important to me was winning. There had been a couple of chances since the Colgate PGA Championship and I was keen to get another win under my belt before the season ended.

I returned to Britain looking forward to making a challenge in the Tournament Players Championship at Foxhills Golf and Country Club in Surrey. But unfortunately I reckon the best way to describe Foxhills, which is a relatively new course, is that it is the best of its kind. The nicest thing about Foxhills that week was that the title went to a really unassuming chap called Brian Waites. He is a club professional from the Notts club at Hollinwell but an extremely fine golfer and whenever he appears on the circuit he can tune in to the pressure of tournament golf. He certainly stood up well to the test that week for he compiled a final round of 69 to come home a 1 stroke winner from defending champion Neil Coles. I was never in the hunt – shooting rounds of 75, 78, 74 and 78.

The following week gave us all a healthy break from the rigorous life of stroke-play tournaments. The Hennessy Cognac Cup matches were being played at The Belfry and I was in the Great Britain and Ireland eleven-man team against the Continent of Europe. This match takes place in alternate years to the Ryder Cup and although it is relatively new, inspired by the progress of the Spanish golfers and the formation of the European Tournament Players Division, it has already proved a worthy addition to the golfing calendar. In fact I'm sure that it is an event which can grow and grow. But it must remain in Britain for it needs the support of our bigger galleries and TV.

The Belfry is a new course designed by Peter Alliss and Dave Thomas. It is also the headquarters of the Professional Golfers Association. To be fair to the course it was rather too new when we played it and so it was possibly too early to form an opinion as to its future. The weather was freezing and you needed your warmest polo-neck in the morning. In fact, that got me into trouble. Tony Gray, one of the ETPD Tournament Directors, gave me a ticking off because he felt that I should be wearing a short-sleeved 'team' shirt! I promised I would try to wear one in the afternoon – but there was no way I wasn't wearing my roll-neck in the mornings. They soon nicknamed The Belfry . . . 'Ice Valley'!

The match was a tight affair with Great Britain and Ireland scampering home by $17\frac{1}{2}$–$14\frac{1}{2}$. It wasn't a bad performance because we had trailed by $6\frac{1}{2}$ to $3\frac{1}{2}$ after the first day and the Continental side included players of the calibre of the Ballesteros brothers, Manuel and Seve, Manuel Pinero, Jose-Maria Canizares, Antonio Garrido and the fast-improving German golfer Bernhard Langer.

It was during the match that I had my third confrontation of the month with Seve. We faced each other in the opening day singles and the game is not remembered so much for the fact that Seve gained quick revenge for the Laurent Perrier episode but for a shot which he produced at the 10th hole. The hole, 310 yards in length, had been constructed so that the golfer must really play 2 shots to the green. It dog-legs to the right, with tall trees blocking the green from the tee and a lake effectively forcing one to hit straight with a medium iron, leaving a deceptive pitch to the green. I was 1 down when we arrived on the 10th and I took out a five-iron and played conservatively down the middle. Now I waited for Seve.

Usually he is right behind and ready to fire away. But this time he was thinking hard and I sensed what was in his mind. When he drew his driver from the bag the crowd shuffled and hushed. Seve was going to try to drive the green. As soon as he struck the ball he knew it was there. He picked up his tee peg without watching the ball. Sure enough it carried the lake and, fading around the trees, came down 8 feet from the hole. A lot of people reckon the shot stunned me and gave Seve the edge to go on and win 2 and 1. That is utter rubbish. I knew that the way Seve was driving the ball that the so-called 'shot-of-the-century' was within his range. The carry was some 280 yards and throughout the year Seve had illustrated he was capable of hitting the ball that far. He had to middle the shot and it needed the right shape, and without any doubt it was a hell of a good shot to pull off. But it didn't shake me.

Looking back, I often wonder what I would have done if Seve had gone first. I'm sure that since it was match-play I would have gone for the green as well and if I had got the right shape in my shot I reckon it would have reached the green. You've got to middle it, that is for sure, but my own view is that a Tom Watson, a Tom Weiskopf, a Ballesteros or a Faldo would all make it 50 per cent of the time. It is certainly a great shot for the crowd to witness.

Unfortunately for the fans, he didn't try it again, but the spectators, who braved the cold, still saw plenty of good action at The Belfry. But they probably didn't realize that on the final day Antonio Garrido and I had a bit of a ding-dong over a couple of incidents during our singles match. Antonio's strength is his steadiness. He rarely makes mistakes and therefore it was clear that it was going to be a stiff contest. We were enjoying a real cut-and-thrust match which got a little hotter when Antonio asked if he could remove a leaf from a bunker. I had to tell him firmly that he couldn't because the rules are that only stones may be removed from sand traps. It seemed to upset him – even though it was the right decision.

Then another incident resulted from an unbelievable putt which I holed at the 14th. He had struck a three-iron so close that I conceded the putt. It left me with a 30 footer for a half. The match was so close that I knew it could turn out to be an important one and so I gave it every chance and the ball dropped into the cup. I was so thrilled and raring to go that I walked to the next tee and drove straight off. It didn't come home to me that since the hole had only been halved it was still Antonio's honour. But halfway down the fairway he turned to me and said that I had played out of turn.

We had to call in George O'Grady, the other ETPD Tournament Director, and ask for a ruling. I was worried that I might lose the hole. I wondered if the match could be given to Antonio. At the best it seemed that I would have to go back to the tee and play another. George, however, told us that the shot can only be replayed if you are called by your opponent on the tee for playing out of turn. So we got on with the game and it went to the last before I won.

Antonio is a great guy and he is not one to hold a grudge. So we were all friends when the match ended. But it illustrated two things. In match-play it is extremely easy to get hot under the collar and we play so little of this type of golf that our knowledge of the rules is not as good as it might be.

It had been a wonderful month for Seve and me in terms of intense competition on and off the course. For Seve, however, The Belfry began a rather controversial period in his career. He had prematurely announced during the Hennessy Cup that he was feeling far from well and that he would not be playing in the second day singles. That was a little embarrassing for Angel Gallardo because, as captain of the side, it was up to him to announce his team day by day. Seve also announced that he would not be playing in the World Cup after representing his country for the last two years and helping to win this trophy for Spain, first with Manuel Pinero and then Antonio Garrido.

All that, however, was rather mild compared to the 'press' that Seve received for the next event – the Dunlop Masters at St Pierre Country Club near Chepstow. Seve was flying back to play after competing in the World Series in America – but he never turned up. Instead, he sent a message to Richard Brown, the Dunlop golf manager, saying that he was unwell and that he was flying straight home from London to Spain. Dunlop made it known that they were deeply upset by Seve's decision and for a while there was some unsavoury talk about his being asked to undergo a medical examination.

Nevertheless, I think the sponsors were more than delighted by the end of the week because Tommy Horton, who plays Dunlop, won the title and the big crowds reflected the attractive field arranged, with stars like Gary Player, Graham Marsh and Peter Oosterhuis all competing. It was nice for Tommy to win because he had suffered on the greens for a couple of years and it was fitting that a tricky 10 foot putt on the last green which he safely holed gave him victory. But I didn't enjoy St Pierre, having to settle for joint twenty-fourth spot.

14
The Wonders of Wentworth

Arnold Palmer. Gary Player. Bob Charles. Jack Nicklaus. Tom Weiskopf. Hale Irwin. David Graham. Graham Marsh. Names to conjure with. All of them greats in their own right. And all of them winners of the World Match Play Championship, a fabulous golfing event which has never failed to capture the public's imagination since it was inaugurated in 1964.

Now I had my second chance to put my name beside the world stars on the victory scroll. I had played in the tournament twelve months earlier and lost to Seve Ballesteros. But I had earned another crack by winning the Colgate PGA Championship earlier in the season. Colgate, who had taken over as sponsors when Piccadilly withdrew after the 1976 event, had brought in a qualifying procedure which included the winner of their other sponsored event. But they had also stuck to the original concept of the World Match Play event.

From the first championship in 1964, it has always been the aim of the sponsors to bring to Wentworth in the autumn of the year the golfing superstars. That is not always easy. Nicklaus, for instance, now brings the curtain down on his season before the end of August. It was now the second week in October. And Lee Trevino, who suffers with a back problem, is aware that the 36 holes a day format in head-to-head combat might be placing too much pressure on his condition.

Nevertheless Colgate gathered at Wentworth this time the US Masters, US Open and US PGA winners. Gary Player, a record five times winner of the World Match Play and entitled to be called 'Mr Wentworth', had taken the Masters with an astonishing final round of 64 at Augusta. Andy North had proved his cool and calculating qualities by holding a four-foot putt to win the US Open when Player, Nicklaus and Tom Watson all threatened at Cherry Hills. And John Mahaffey had found the light at the end of a long, personal dark tunnel by beating Watson and Jerry Pate in a play-off for the US PGA at Oakmont.

Watson, who had come so close throughout the season to winning more 'majors' following his successes in the US Masters and British Open in 1977, was also in the field. So were previous winners Graham Marsh and David Graham, both Australians, Ray Floyd, Lee Elder and Andy Bean from the States and Isao Aoki from Japan. And the European circuit was represented by Seve, South African Dale Hayes, New Zealander Simon Owen and my compatriots Mark James and Brian Waites.

It was a galaxy of stars that was certain to attract another capacity crowd to this annual showpiece. The format of the championship – match-play contests over 36 holes – has ensured the World Match Play event has established a unique place in golfing history. It appears to possess a magnetic hold on the golf fans. Wentworth in October can be rough and windy and wet. It can be foggy and cold. Yet the spectators clamour for tickets and even when the weather is unkind there hardly seems room on the tree-lined fairways for them to walk. Miniature cardboard periscopes pop up all over the place as the owners peer over the heads of fellow spectators. Boys sit straddled on fathers' shoulders to get a glimpse of the action. For at Wentworth in the World Match Play a single shot can dramatically change the destiny of a particular match.

Peter Alliss, a former Ryder Cup player but now better known to the golfing fraternity as a television commentator, aptly described the glamour and respect that the World Match Play Championship has gained. He compared it to 'Wimbledon, the final Test at Lord's, the last night at the Proms – an event to attend, to be seen at, a place where companies could entertain their customers right royally.' Some have subscribed to a belief that the World Match Play is the fifth 'major' championship. Some say that is being over-generous to an event without the historical claims of the Open. Yet outside of the Open, there is no event in the world that I would rather win.

I must admit that from a player's point of view it is a very special week. For we are the 'house guests' of the sponsors. They arrange private houses on the affluent Wentworth estate. For a week the player is the 'boss' in luxurious houses of enormous character. He can have his wife and members of their families with him, and can invite guests for dinner. A chauffeur-driven car is at his disposal for the entire week. It arrives to take the player to the course, and the house guests can go shopping. Indeed, you lead the life of a lord! And if you are fortunate enough to win the tournament you also take home a rather handsome reward . . . £30,000.

I began the week in the worst possible way. I drove back from St Pierre on the previous Saturday evening and arrived home in good time to have a light supper and get to bed nice and early. We had asked for the chauffeur-driven Mercedes to arrive first thing on Sunday to take us to Wentworth. I wanted to get in some early practice over Wentworth's Burma Road course. But the car didn't arrive. We waited for half an hour or so and then telephoned the Colgate officials at the course to let them know. It seemed quite possible that the driver could have lost his way, since our house is tucked away in the Hertfordshire countryside.

That turned out not to be the case. The driver had gone to the house at Wentworth where we were due to stay. There had been a misunderstanding and when I had called and asked to be picked up from the house they assumed that I was already on the estate. So it seemed ridiculous to ask the car to come out at that stage. Instead I drove down to Wentworth myself and took it from there.

There was a bonus, because when I eventually met the driver – Don – he turned out to be a great guy. Golfers are a peculiar breed in as much as we have our own prearranged timetables with regard to arriving at a course, practising and playing. We like it to go according to plan every time or somehow it seems that we're not quite in the groove. So it is important to have a driver who is going to be punctual. Don was more than that. He used to arrive half an hour early just to make sure. It meant that I was always at the course in good time to prepare for the day's play.

I suppose it is impossible to be unlucky with the allocation of houses since they are all magnificent. But we were extremely fortunate as our hostess, Molly Neilson, remained at home, where she prepared fabulous food for us. Molly is a cordon bleu cook and it was great to be able to invite a couple of guests round in the evening to sample her culinary delights.

So the scene was set for a super week. My mum and dad came down to stay in the house, which made it feel as if it was home sweet home. I felt I needed a few things in my favour since my first-round opponent was Andy Bean. He brought with him a big reputation. It wasn't so much that he had won three US events and gathered $267,241 for third place in their money list. It was more that he arrived in Britain as a kind of fairy-tale giant. He was 6 feet 4 inches tall and weighed 15 stone. He was reputed to have crushed a golf ball with his teeth and once to have wrestled with alligators. With that kind of physique and muscle I was considerably concerned about the distance he could knock a ball !

In that kind of situation it would be relatively easy to be frightened from the start. Let's face it, Andy Bean carried a reputation for big hitting which threatened to turn Wentworth's tough par 4s into drive and wedge holes. So, if somebody can reduce the length of the Burma Road in that manner, he must be fancied to win. Yet it is a fact that Wentworth, enclosed by trees, can have a crushing effect on the big hitters and sometimes they become so preoccupied with keeping out of trouble that their length from the tee is severely cut and their game suffers. So I fancied myself to win the first round.

Initially, it all went really well. I went out and knocked it past him at the 1st, 2nd and 4th holes. In fact, it made me think that, perhaps, I struck the ball further than most. Then we arrived on the 9th tee, a 460 yard hole which demands that the drive be struck straight and solid in order to carry a blanket of gorse and bracken. You need really to blast it here and that is just what Andy did. His ball sailed no fewer than 30 yards past mine. It was incredible. And it was the kind of shot which suggested Andy might outpower me at the long 17th and 18th holes and nick, so to speak, the initiative immediately before lunch.

Astonishingly, exactly the opposite happened. I arrived at the 16th tee 1 up and went in to lunch 4 up. There is absolutely no doubt that this particular first-round match was decided there and then. In truth, Andy handed me a couple of holes by 3 putting both the 16th and 17th, but I birdied the 502 yard dog-leg 18th to send him leaden-chinned in to lunch. 4 up. I felt quietly confident.

It was not too long before Andy showed that he was not going to go down without a fight. He won the 2nd and 5th holes in the afternoon session to cut my lead in half. But I countered quickly and effectively by winning the 6th and 8th and Andy found himself 4 down again with only 10 holes remaining. As a contest the match probably ceased once we made the turn for the final time. It ended at the 14th where I struck a solid four-iron into the green to set up a 5 and 4 success.

Simon Owen and Ray Floyd both won their first-round matches by similar margins – beating Andy North and John Mahaffey respectively. But the biggest win was gained by hot favourite Tom Watson. He produced golf of the highest calibre, covering the first 18 holes in an incredible 65, to murder poor Dale Hayes by a tournament record 11 and 9. It was a success which convinced all the other survivors that Watson was undoubtedly the man to beat that week. Yet he lasted only to the second round because Ray Floyd edged him out by a 2 hole margin in a match which thrilled the gallery, since between them they were 20 under par. Watson even managed to keep the game going with an eagle 3 at the 17th (35th) hole before Floyd gained his place among the semi-finalists.

I spent the evening before the second round enjoying a quiet meal at the house and pondering the exciting possibility of being £30,000 richer in three days' time. The confidence stemmed largely from my conclusive triumph over Andy Bean, but it was boosted by the knowledge that I had the partisan Wentworth gallery right behind me. The applause I was given on my way back to the clubhouse following the win over Bean was astounding. So, with Mark James being narrowly beaten by Seve, and Brian Waites also being removed, I was left to carry the flag for Britain and it seemed certain that there would be plenty of support. My game was also solid and my putting stroke felt good. I slept well.

When we gathered at the clubhouse for the second round it was obvious that play would be delayed. The 'Wentworth fog' had descended. You could hardly see across the road, some 30 yards from the 1st tee, let alone the fairway. It was a case of waiting for the fog to lift. We waited, and waited and waited. You begin to get edgy. It is simply that I had got myself ready to play – and all that was on my mind was beating Graham Marsh. The much-travelled Australian had beaten Brian Waites to earn his place in the second round and as the defending champion he was a very formidable opponent.

The time ticked on and there was no improvement in the conditions. What to do? There is a limit to how long you can stand on the putting green practising. I went to sit in the car and listened to a few music tapes. It was clear that a point was being reached where the tournament officials would need to make a decision on whether or not play was going to take place. Then they acted. The fog had lifted sufficiently by midday for us to have time to play 18 holes. The other 18 would be played the next day, Saturday, and the semi-finals would now take place on Sunday, with the final on Monday.

In my opinion, we should not have played at all that day. I consider the entire 36 holes should have been played on the Saturday. The officials had pushed back the semi-finals and final, so why not the second round? And the result of the decision to play just 18 holes upset my balance. I'm positive that I was not ready to play. My game was not as sharp as it might have been and my concentration was poor. The result? I was 4 down to Graham at the end of the first 18 holes.

It is terrible trying to play on a day when you have no feel or judgement. I knew I couldn't return to the house in my current state of mind. So, with the fog closing in again, I made my way to the practice ground. I was hoping to leave the course with the knowledge that my game was sharp. So that I could sleep that night not feeling like a condemned man, but with my confidence restored. In no way had I given up. It was an uphill job – but tomorrow was another day.

There were other great players in my position. Watson was at that point 3 down to Floyd. Player surprisingly trailed Aoki by a similar margin. Ballesteros was 1 down to Owen. Watson, Player, Ballesteros – they all promised revivals. I wanted to upstage all of them – and come back from 4 down. I went out on the Saturday determined to charge the course – to give it everything I had. The break had given me a chance to get a second wind and my strategy was simple – all-out attack. I knew it would be useless to sit back and wait for Graham to make mistakes. I had to force him into a situation where he had to play positively. I had been cautious during the first round against Bean. Ian Connelly, my coach, wanted me to use my driver more. Now I had to – in spite of the tight fairways of Wentworth. There could be no holding back.

By the turn, the crowd sensed that I might be able to pull it off. I won the 8th and then at the 9th Graham drove into a tiny water hazard on the right. It seemed certain to be my hole. But Graham realized that the time was ripe to employ a little gamesmanship. I've been told that he saw me standing on the other side of the fairway rarin' to go. Of course, he was right. I could feel my big chance coming. But Graham, instead of taking a penalty drop and getting straight on with it, chose to walk slowly back to the tee to play another ball. It was a pointless decision because he knew he would lose the hole. But there seems little doubt that he wanted to upset my rhythm.

Three holes later he employed a similar technique. He hooked the ball into the trees, spent some time unsuccessfully searching for it, then called the referee for a prolonged chat on whether or not he was going to play a provisional ball. It all got very complicated. But on neither occasion did it disturb my concentration. And by winning the 9th and then the 12th I had cut my deficit to 1.

At that point I don't think there was a thought of defeat in my head. I reckoned Graham was on the rack and I was ready to turn it so that it hurt. But in the end a lady's heel came to his rescue. At the 16th he squirted his drive out to the right. I was down the middle and it looked as if the match would be square with 2 to play. But Graham's ball struck the shoe of a lady spectator and bounced back on to the fairway. If the ball had kept going right there is no way he could have got his second shot close to the pin. Instead, he was able to take out a four-iron and he drilled an immaculate shot to 8 feet. The putt never looked like missing and, instead of being all square, he was 2 up.

It was a bitter blow. But I realized the crowd were doing everything to lift me. I recalled how many times Gary Player had found himself in such predicaments at Wentworth and turned defeat into victory. At the 571 yard 17th, there is out of bounds on the left, so it is not a hole you can generally attack. Indeed, if you go out of bounds, you are in the garden of one of the houses backing on to the course. I knew that if I went out of bounds it would be all over. So I drove from the tee with respect rather than recklessness. Then I hit a glorious second, chipped to 18 feet and holed the putt to be 1 down with 1 to play. Now I could still win.

I'll always believe that I was unlucky at the last. I struck a good drive and went for the green with a three-wood. In my mind was the thought that an eagle 3 would do the trick. My second shot was good and it looked as if it must finish within 10 feet. But it hit the front of the green and pulled up sharply. Graham was short in 2, but now there was not quite so much pressure on him. He chipped to 6 feet. To make sure of a sudden-death play-off I needed to hole from 30 feet. The ball shaved the hole but it didn't drop and Graham gratefully conceded and holed his own putt. He had won by 1 hole.

Graham later said that he felt that the match was slipping away. The fact is I was 6 under for the day and it annoyed me to think that without that fog the previous day I might have made it to the semi-finals. The other semi-finalists were Owen, a 150–1 bet at the start of the week, Aoki, priced at 33–1, and Floyd, who was 10–1. The favourites – Watson, Ballesteros and Player – had all been beaten. Four were left to battle for £30,000 first prize – and I wasn't involved.

Aoki, once a 25p-a-round caddie, had the honourable distinction of becoming the first Japanese player to win a major international title outside his own country. He overcame Owen 3 and 2 in the final. Owen, runner-up to Nicklaus earlier in the year in the Open Championship, had the satisfaction of beating North, Ballesteros and Marsh on the way and earning a satisfying cheque for £18,000.

But I'll always know that a lady's heel quite possibly cost me the chance of beating Marsh and going on for a crack at the title.

15
Walton Heath Blues

Cameramen! You can love 'em and hate 'em. I love the thought that the cameras are following me at a top tournament – because it almost certainly means I'm in contention. As a rule they don't bother me. You know that they are there and you accept that millions of people could be watching you back home on TV. But at the European Open on 18 October I was livid with a bunch of cameramen – and I reckon that I had every reason to be.

It was the first round of the European Open, a new tournament on the calendar, and, although I could no longer overhaul Seve at the top of the Order of Merit, I was absolutely determined that the jackpot £18,000 top cheque would be in my bank at the end of the week. It was the end of the season and it would have been easy to have simply gone into the event and tried my best. But following my departure at Wentworth I had returned to see Ian Connelly and work hard on my swing. We had three two-hour sessions in order to obtain a better take-away and back swing. The result was that I teed-off knowing that I was striking the ball solidly enough to win.

And after four hours of intense play around the 7130 yards Walton Heath course I arrived at the 18th hole requiring a 30 foot birdie putt for a 3 stroke lead. Everything had gone according to plan, because I was partnered by Tom Weiskopf and I felt confident that I could get the right tempo from him. In fact, I stole his rhythm on the front 9 to such an extent that over the back half I was playing almost my best golf of the year. I holed well from 8 feet for a birdie 3 at the 10th and then rather more nicely from 25 feet for an eagle 3 at the monster

507 yard 11th. Then I collected two more birdies with putts
of 8 at the 15th and 17th.

So there I was, on the 18th green, facing a 30 foot putt which
would take me 3 strokes clear of American Lon Hinkle,
Australian Greg Norman and Spaniard Manuel Calero. They
had all shot 69s and I needed this putt for 66. I felt good. I
felt confident. I felt as if I had already made the putt. By the
time that I had weighed up the line and the strength of touch
required to get to the hole a hush had descended over the
crowd in the grandstand which surrounded the green. I
addressed the putt. I was ready to go and then . . . *crash!* . . .
and a yell: 'Oh my back, you'll have to watch it, Bill.'

It was unbelievable. A camera crew, in a golf buggy, had
driven round behind me. The buggy had gone over a bump
and one of the passengers had banged his back and it was he
who had shouted. I know that it must have hurt him. But
the staggering thing was that the buggy was still moving. They
seemed to be trying to get into a new position but with scant
regard for me. I went to address the putt again, but out of
the corner of my eye I saw that the buggy was on the move
again. One chap said to another, 'We've got him now. That's
him over there – make sure you're in focus.' To some people
it must have seemed like a Charlie Chaplin comedy. Then the
next second a newspaper seller walked straight across the back
of the green.

The headline across the back page of the *Daily Express* the
next day read: FALDO IS FURIOUS – TV CREW ROW CUTS LEAD.
Furious? I was seething. I went over to the cameramen and
demanded, 'Is there anything wrong with you?'

One of them answered, 'No, nothing.'

So I replied, 'Well, great.' To be fair, it is the kind of situation you should not allow to affect you. As I've said, Ian
Connelly instilled in me early in my career the importance of
remaining cool and calm amid such disturbances. But on this
occasion I felt something had to be said. It was not like a
spectator coughing unexpectedly at a critical moment. Or
another accidentally dropping his shooting stick. These chaps
were making a real meal of it.

I had worked hard all the way round. I didn't want to throw
shots away at this point – but after the disturbance I 3 putted

and finished with 68 and a 1 stroke lead. Some critics claimed afterwards that I used the incident as an excuse for 3 putting. Absolute rubbish. There were a few people on the spot at the time and I asked their opinion. All agreed with me that the television crew made a shattering noise. I accept they had their job to do – but it seems to me a decision was taken too late to get the crew into position.

The outcome was that it ruined what could have been an excellent round. If the score on my card at the end of the day had been 66 I would have been in position A to run away from the field – just as I had in the Colgate. That's the kind of opportunity you definitely don't want to see disappear just when it seems within your grasp. But now that had happened.

It also struck me that 66 – and at worse 67 – would have been a really excellent round over the Walton Heath course. The circuit we played for the European Open was a composite 18 holes taken from the New and Old Courses. In the main we were playing the Old but the 12th, 13th and 18th had been taken from the New. It had been arranged this way because the European Open was a big affair – a £100,000 prize fund – and the sponsors were hoping that huge crowds would flock to the Surrey course. There was certainly a number of good reasons for making the trip. Several top Americans had flown in, including Gil Morgan, Bobby Wadkins, Lou Graham, Ed Sneed, Al Geiberger, Lon Hinkle, Mac McLendon and Tom Weiskopf.

In 1973 at Troon I stood for hours watching Weiskopf play. I marvelled at his silky smooth swing. The entire action was simply one piece. He looked to have everything going for him and victory in the Open seemed a mere formality. In fact, he came home 3 shots ahead of Neil Coles and Johnny Miller. He returned to America as the Open Champion and I returned to Welwyn with a picture in my mind of the rhythm which gave him his super swing. So it was great to get the chance to partner Tom at Walton Heath and it seemed rather strange to be ahead of him. But I knew that the second day could be critical – with Tom burning to charge at me. I also had to pick myself up following that crushing 18th hole incident.

I missed breakfast on the morning of the second round – and went to work on a Mars bar! But I also went to work on

A drive at St Andrews; a session on the practice putting green; and a studious look at Tony Jacklin.

Ian Connelly, one of the country's top teaching professionals, who fired my ambition and gave me the confidence to go out and win.

sink a long putt – and *(right)* retrieve the ball after holing-in-one at the 191 yard 17th at Walton Heath in the third round of the European Open.

Early days and dreams of being a champion; reality in May, 1978, and victory in the Colgate PGA Championship.

Walking a course in South Africa with my wife, Melanie – and saluting
the winning putt in the ICL International at Kensington.

A 1977 Ryder Cup trio – captain Brian Huggett, Tony Jacklin and
Mark James.

copying Tom. And it worked so well. There was a point in the round when I felt that I was beginning to swing badly. The rhythm was deserting me. We had a kind of match-play situation going with Tom fighting me for the lead. The pressure was boiling up and it was imperative that I made as few mistakes as possible. So I stood back for a minute and just watched Tom swing the club. I noted the way he completed the backswing and I remembered to do exactly the same myself. Immediately I felt back on song – the crispness was there and I was prepared to ward off Tom's attack.

He had drawn level at the 11th but I never allowed him to sneak ahead, and at the end of the day my 70 for a total of 138 gave me a 1 shot edge on Tom, who was round in 69. Greg Norman was 2 strokes further back and 1 ahead of a group of eight players.

The surprising aspect of the second round was the failure of Seve to make the halfway cut. In the first round he had suffered the blow of 'losing' his clubs and he used a borrowed set from the local professional. That led to an uncharacteristic 75 – and the irony of the whole affair was that he heard on the 6th green that his clubs had been found. 'Where?' asked Seve. 'In a member's locker in the clubhouse,' came the answer.

It seemed that Seve presumed his caddie had looked after the clubs overnight, but they had been left against the wall of the clubhouse and a locker-room attendant put them into the member's locker for safe keeping! Seve could have stayed in the event with a good second round but he took 41 strokes on the back 9 and his total of 153 – 15 shots behind me – was too many.

So with my rival of 1978 out of the way and my game nice and solid I went into the third round feeling good. Within twenty minutes of teeing off I was fighting a battle to claw myself back into the event following the biggest 1 hole disaster of my entire season. I ran up an 8 at the 513 yard 2nd where they say the tee is no place for the timid golfer and boldness must be the correct strategy. The reason? Out of bounds on the left and a bunker on the right, which can intimidate the best golfer.

My game plan for the week had been to strike the drive down

the left but with a fade so that the ball worked its way back to the centre of the fairway. When trouble – like out of bounds – lurks, you must take extra care and the professional way is to aim where the problem lies but with a shot that takes the ball out of harm's way. But on the third day, as we walked to the tee, my caddie kept talking to me about that bunker on the right. He insisted that in the conditions that day it represented the most lethal problem. So I reached the tee in two minds – should I stick to the original shot or aim at the bunker with a draw and take the ball into the fairway that way? I went for the latter, over-cooked it and the ball whistled out of bounds. It was a stunning blow. My next drive went into the heather and I eventually finished with 8 on my card.

In such cases, you cannot attach blame to anybody but yourself. It is true that the caddie's comments swayed my mind into thinking that a drawing shot would be the best. But I struck the ball. And I hit it out of bounds. It had happened – an eight was on my card and now it was up to me to get back into the game. I would have to fight all the way if that £18,000 was to remain my target.

I buckled down to the task ahead, but dropped another shot at the 5th, then birdied the 6th and 7th as this astonishing day in my golfing career continued. Bogey 5s at the 8th and 10th followed but ten minutes later I was on another 'high' after reducing the 507 yard dog-leg 11th to a drive and a two-iron and rapping home a putt of no less than 25 feet for a morale-boosting eagle 3. It should have helped me back into contention, but the shots were frittered away again with bogeys at the 12th and 14th.

It was beginning to look bleak and, although poor Tom Weiskopf had dropped out of it with the recurrence of an old wrist injury, I knew that something special was needed over the last few holes if there was to be a glimmer of hope for my own winning chances. Australian Greg Norman, my third-round partner, was steering a confident course along the Walton Heath track and, with his compatriot David Graham and ex-Ryder Cup star Malcolm Gregson also making significant progress, there was a lot for me to do. How I wished it had been possible to return to play that second hole again! But it was over and my only escape route was to turn the closing holes into a triumphant march. A birdie at the 15th was a marvellous start but it was the 191 yard 17th which gave me the lifeline I so desperately required.

Greg hit first at the 17th, but after he had struck his tee shot there was a tremendous commotion. What happened was that a chap unfortunately collapsed behind the tee and a lot of people swarmed round to see if they could help him out. He clearly needed attention – but not the attention of the TV cameramen. Yet the guys with the camera were trying to force their way through to capture the poor man's agony. It was quite ridiculous and Greg Norman took it on himself to stop the action. He calmly walked over and pulled a cameraman away and told him that he should concentrate on the golf. It was a nice thing for Greg to do and I'm sure the spectator would have been pleased that Greg made sure that the scene was not shown on the screen. Finally I pulled a six-iron out of my bag, fired the ball at the green and watched in sheer amazement as the ball bounced straight into the hole for an ace!

I couldn't believe it. What a freaky round I had experienced. An 8, an eagle 3, a bunch of bogeys and birdies and a hole-in-one. It seemed highly likely that something out of this world must happen at the 18th and the thought crossed my mind that perhaps I could hole my second shot for a sizzling eagle 2. But it was not to be the case, for I pulled my approach to the green and carded another bogey 5. I had finished with 75 for a score of 213. It was not so bad as it might have been after that tragic start, but it left me 3 shots behind Greg Norman. He was on 210 – 2 strokes ahead of David Graham and Malcolm Gregson. There was still everything to play for, but I went to the practice ground cursing that 8.

It was now coming towards the end of October and the nights were drawing in, but I wandered over to the practice ground to employ the remaining minutes of daylight usefully. There was not too much wrong with my game, but it was important to ensure that I returned in the morning with that 8 firmly ruled out of my mind and my confidence high. I woke up to find that I had made the front page of the *Sunday Express* with a 'Nick holes in one' story. I was smiling and now it dawned on me that, although there had been no prize for the ace, it was quite conceivable that the hole-in-one could propel me towards the title.

There can be little doubt that the first European Open produced one of the most enthralling finales of the 1978 golf season. Bobby Wadkins, one of the lesser-known American faces at that time, had started that last day trailing Greg Norman by no fewer than 5 strokes. Yet it was 27-year-old Bobby, who was forty-sixth on the United States money list at that time, who came through to set the pace for the rest of the field. He reached the turn in a 3 under par 33, then seemed to throw away his chance of collecting the magnificent trophy. He dropped shots at the 10th – known as 'Cotton's Hole' because Henry Cotton once drove across the corner to the front of the green to win it with a birdie 3 in a challenge match – and then the 12th. Yet he eagled the 14th and birdied the 16th and 17th to come home in 68 for a 9 under par total of 283. Now Bobby had to sit in the clubhouse while we all attacked his score.

I was desperately trying to launch my bid for victory, but there seemed to be no way for me to get things going. I was just plodding along nicely without getting the right results. I strung together a number of good shots to set up the birdie chances, but the putts refused to drop. There was one that lipped out from 12 feet when it seemed certain that the ball was in the cup. At the 15th I hit my approach with a seven-iron to 10 feet but missed the putt. At the 16th I struck a long four-iron to 15 feet but the ball lipped out again. Now, at the short 17th, the hope was that I could get an ace again and, although it was not to be, the next best thing happened and a birdie 2 went down on my card.

That left a really interesting situation. It meant that my two partners on that final day – Malcolm Gregson and American Mac McLendon – and myself all needed to birdie the 397 yard par 4 last hole to tie Wadkins for the lead. We all reached the green in two, but I failed from 30 feet, McLendon from 20 feet and Gregson from 18 feet. It gave Mac and myself 71s and Malcolm a 72 and we were all on 284 – one behind Wadkins. Now it was all over for me and I walked slowly and downcast from the scorer's caravan.

Meanwhile as Bobby Wadkins waited in the clubhouse, out

on the course a bunch of players were still seeking the key to overhauling his total. He had survived our challenge, but he received a monumental jolt when Bernard Gallacher birdied the 517 yard 14th to go 9 under, and be on level-pegging. American Gil Morgan, too, was piling on the pressure, and although he missed a good birdie chance at the 17th Gil had made $267,000 in the States that year and you win that kind of money by making those kind of putts. In it went and now the two Americans waited to see what else would happen on this adventurous afternoon.

After Jerry McGee had narrowly failed with a 68 for 285 and Ed Sneed and Brian Barnes had shot 68s for 286, it came down to Gallacher or Greg Norman troubling the pacesetters. Greg was not really at his best, and although he had a chance from 12 feet to force a tie he failed to make it and a 74 put him on the same score as myself. Meanwhile Bernard had looked all over a winner at the 16th and 17th where on both occasions he struck solid putts. But they stayed out and now, still at 9 under, he needed a birdie at the last to win. His drive was unbelievable – he topped it – and with thousands of people watching he had to grit his teeth in typically grim fashion and fight for the 4 which eventually earned him a play-off with the Americans. But really Bernard had lost his chance over those last 3 holes.

The first extra hole decided the title. The 460 yard 16th was played and Wadkins, following a superb three-iron to 3 feet, won it with a birdie 3 to the 4 of Gallacher and the 5 of Morgan. Bernard had a chance from 6 feet but he failed and so Bobby Wadkins had taken the European Open – ironically about the same time as his brother Lanny was winning the Victorian PGA title at Woodlands in Australia. So Bobby picked up the £18,000 top prize and I was left clutching a consolation cheque for £3543. I had really felt that the European Open was destined to go the same way as the Colgate PGA Championship earlier in the year when I ran away from the field. But looking back that 8 really proved to be an insurmountable handicap when fighting to keep in contention.

The 1978 European season was over. I had to be content with third spot in the Order of Merit. Seve had topped the 'league' for the third successive season and this time he registered official winnings of £54,348. Dale Hayes of South Africa was second with £43,890 and I was the top home player with £37,911. It was a nice feeling that at the ripe old age of 21 (!) I had proved myself in the company of such outstanding players as Tony Jacklin, Neil Coles, Tommy Horton, Brian Barnes and Bernard Gallacher. I had come out on top and in front of a number of tremendous young players like Ken Brown, Mark James and Howard Clark.

Yet I was not completely satisfied. I had done well but when the season began my ambition had been to win tournaments – not merely one – and to finish at the top of the Order of Merit. People say you cannot win every week but I think you can expect to be in contention all the time. I believe I should never be out of the running. Winning one week makes me want to win the next. Stop winning – and you lose the habit.

16
Good Golly! Nick Faldo

John Simpson is the man who handles all my business affairs. He works for Mark H. McCormack's International Management Group in London. So he is part of a massive world-wide operation which Mark has built up since he elected to take a back seat from his chosen profession as a lawyer and instead work with and for Arnold Palmer and promote individuals and the game of golf.

Mark now represents a host of sporting stars including Arnold, Gary Player and Tony Jacklin in golf; skier Jean-Claude Killy; tennis stars Bjorn Borg, John Newcombe, Virginia Wade and Evonne Cawley; and former world motor-racing champion Jackie Stewart. Mark was once described as 'the Unofficial Chancellor of the Exchequer of Professional Golf'. But with such a huge empire 'Chancellor Mark' must delegate responsibility to a massive work-force spread across the world. John Simpson is his man in London when it comes to looking after the European golfers.

But John is more than just a manager. He is a great friend. We met a year before he joined the International Management Group when I was competing in the Penfold PGA Championship at Royal St George's in Kent. I was unaware that John had seen me play once before – back in my amateur days in the Berkshire Trophy. That we came to meet was probably a spot of good fortune for both of us because we immediately struck up a friendship which has developed to the extent that we are almost considered brothers. In fact John was my best man when I married Melanie.

We came to meet because John Moorhouse, my caddie,

and I were staying with the parents of a friend – John Powell
– at their home in Broadstairs. The two Johns had grown up
together and played golf at the nearby North Foreland club
and I had met John Powell during my amateur days. When
we all got together in that week of the Penfold we just seemed
to click and we had a really fun week. I'm sure that it helped
me relax in the tournament when I had to play in the company
of Gary Player and I finished with 69 for joint sixth place and
one of my biggest cheques up to that point – for £1625.

At the time John Simpson was working in public relations
for Hilderstone, an adult training centre, which I understand
is the only profit-making organization on the teaching side in
the Kent County Council. It followed a spell in the family
hotel business at Broadstairs, after he had obtained a degree
in business studies at Westminster College in London.

John possesses tremendous perception. But when he phoned
me at home one morning after joining the McCormack organization and told me that I was going to make money out of
being a 'golly' I thought he had gone crazy. It was breakfast
time and John had been spreading his toast with Robertsons
marmalade and the thought struck him that as a boy he had
sent in for their Golly badges, one of which showed the Golly-
wog with a golf club. He reckoned Robertsons might be
interested in some kind of contract which benefited both them
and me. But poor John did not know what he was letting
himself in for.

John joined the International Management Group only a
week after I had won the Colgate PGA Championship at Royal
Birkdale. I had put a word in for him, but in the end that
hindered rather than helped his chances. The fact was that the
top people in the London office were terrified that John would
just look after 'yours truly' and that he would forget that the
job required advising a whole band of golfers. So, since there
were a number of candidates for the position, John had to
present a strong case for being given the opportunity. But he
was given the position and he set to work to prove himself.

It would be fair to say that since I had just won the Colgate
I was what is termed a hot property. My name had been on
the front pages of the national press and I was a marketing
commodity. I couldn't be compared with the greats like

Nicklaus, Palmer, Watson and Player, but in Europe I was being labelled as the rival to Spanish superstar Seve Ballesteros. So John knew he was not going to get any complaints from the big boys in the London office for concentrating on obtaining a few new contracts for me. Now all he had to do was go out and sell me.

So after our breakfast-time chat on the phone, which left me chuckling, he made off to the office very boldly and ready to start business with Robertsons. He was new. He was learning. He was using his own initiative. And the first phone call to Robertsons seemed to put him at ease. He was told to come for a meeting at Beckenham. But John will never forget that day for three reasons. First he began to get the shakes the nearer he got to Beckenham. He had never dealt with a company that big before and how was he going to sell a golfer to a jam manufacturer?

John tells the story better than I, but it seems he was ushered into this palatial boardroom and introduced to Mr Christopher. John shook hands firmly and replied, 'How do you do, Mr Christopher.' In fact he was talking to Mr Christopher Robertson, the chairman. John laughs about it now, but he openly admits that the incident did little to steady his nerves at the time. But by the time he left the boardroom he was able to phone me up and say 'Good Golly, Nick Faldo . . . we've got a deal.' But there can be little doubt that it was a tough starter for John and he did well to pass with flying colours.

Some people might think that the marketing of top sportsmen and women, or a so-called superstar, is easy. But it certainly is not. Nobody picks up a phone and calls your manager and says, 'Hi, I've got £5000 I want to give to Nick Faldo.' The manager has to get out and sell. He has to possess the inspiration to think of new contracts. The deal with Robertsons suited them at the time and in return for a contract I displayed a Golly on my golf bag and carried a Golly umbrella. I also took part in company days for them where you meet and play with members and guests of Robertsons. That, basically, is how it all works.

When John arrived at IMG in London I already possessed a very good golf-clubs deal with the Ram company. In fact, Mark McCormack set that one up himself because it had been arranged in America after he completed a 'package deal' with Colgate-Palmolive, who were widening their sporting interests under the leadership of David Foster. Colgate were running the Penfold PGA Championship in Britain and the company later assumed sponsorship of the World Match Play Championship when Carreras Rothmans pulled out. I was part of the deal as an up-and-coming player.

My connection with IMG stemmed from a meeting in 1975 with Jeremy Ward, who worked for them at that time. It was rather strange because I was in the middle of my good year as an amateur and a couple of pressmen approached me and asked if anybody from IMG had spoken to me about the future. In fact, only twenty-four hours later Jeremy phoned me and he simply told me about IMG and that he was there any time I wanted to have a chat. I guess at the time they were not really interested, but like a good businessman Jeremy was keeping in contact just in case they needed to make a quick approach. But I was advised by a lot of different people not to be too hasty and to wait until I was a fully fledged professional before making a decision.

During the next twelve months, I could hardly believe the number of people who came forward to talk to me. It seemed best to allow my father to chat to them all so that my golf game was not affected by such distractions. Vinnie Giles, the top American amateur who had entered the managerial world, was one who was interested. So was Bruce Streather. In fact Bruce helped me to get to Houston University and he did all the paper-work. I met another chap, James Marshall, along with my father and mother, and he offered me a deal which, on turning professional, would mean that I would have enough money to cover all my expenses and that I could keep all the prize money. But he wanted the contract to run five years – that was much too long.

There were other managerial types who came around for a chat and to be quite frank I enjoyed the excitement of being a 'wanted man' and it enabled me to gain an insight into the sponsorship business. The important thing to learn is that it's impossible to sell yourself. It is a specialist's job and anyway I would never be any good haggling over pounds, shillings and pence. So you must have a manager who has your best interests at heart – and a manager, in my opinion, is always better than a sponsor. What can happen with a sponsor is that he will offer you all your expenses and, perhaps, a cheque book, and you use him as a bank. That would be perfectly OK in one respect if it actually worked that way. But too often it does not. Instead, you find that the money you win goes back into the bank and that there is some kind of percentage arrangement wrapped up in the contract. And if you don't get asked for the money back at the end of the year it is conceivable that if you start to do well the chap will arrive on your doorstep four or five years later and say, 'Remember me . . . ? Well this is what our contract stated . . .'

My theory is that if you have the confidence and if you are prepared to work hard you will be rewarded. I guess people could turn round and say that it is easy for me to talk like this since I now have no financial worries. But it is not long ago that I had no money. However, I did possess confidence in my own ability to reach the top. I was £600 in the red, and my father, who helped me so much throughout my amateur career, had to admit that the well was running dry. We could have weakened then and looked for a full-time sponsor. But to me that would have been admitting defeat. I was determined that after getting that far under our own steam we would have the benefits when I struck golfing oil.

In the end, I selected the International Management Group to organize my affairs because of a unique arrangement struck in August 1976. George Blumberg, who had helped me so much when I was in South Africa and had given me advice whenever I needed it, phoned me and told me not to make a single move. He said that he was coming to Britain for the Open Championship at Royal Birkdale and that we should have a long discussion on the subject of managers. He is a personal friend of Mark McCormack, and, of course, he was probably keen that I should join IMG. But at the same time 'Uncle George', as I called him, wanted to see everything done fairly. He did not want to see me in an arrangement which would not suit me and might interfere with my golfing progress.

George went off for a chat with Mark and he returned to tell me that Mark had given his word that he would handle me for a trial period of six months. It meant that at the end of the year I was free to go my own way if I was not hitting it off with the people at IMG. I could just say thank you and leave. The great thing was having somebody I could trust. I had met George when I travelled to South Africa as part of the British Commonwealth team in 1975. Gerald Micklem and George communicate quite often and Gerald suggested that George take a look at me. It was that meeting which led to my staying with George in South Africa in 1976 at the start of my professional career.

Now I have the same kind of trust with John Simpson. I must admit that our relationship can change now that he is looking after my business affairs. There are times when I make decisions which, quite frankly, do not bring a smile to John's face. But I respect that he has a job to do and that I must listen to his advice. He is there to help me and lift any aggravation from my shoulders so that I can concentrate on my golf.

John helps to plan my programme. It is not just a case of working out which tournament in Europe I want to play. There might be an invitation to the US Masters, as in 1979, and you must carefully plan the arrangements so that you are not playing too much golf, travelling for too long and getting stale. There are also trips to places like Australia, Japan and South Africa to work out.

John knows that if I play well in far away places he has the opportunity to 'sell me', so to speak, in those countries. There is a limit to the number of contracts one can obtain in Britain and, to a lesser extent, in Europe. For instance you can only be tied to one club manufacturer and to one clothing company. But John has successfully hunted for other endorsements.

In the last few years there has been a trend for affiliations to switch from golf clubs to companies. So I now represent Glynwed, giant bathroom and kitchen company. They make everything from taps to Aga cookers. But, more importantly, Glynwed and I have struck a superb relationship. Their chairman, Mr Fletcher, is a tremendous guy and we often meet and have a chat at the golf tournaments. In return for my name being attached to Glynwed I offer them several days a year in order to play golf with the directors and clients. The name Glynwed is also on my golf bag and it appears behind my name in all tournament programmes.

I accept that I was very lucky at the start to have a contract with Ram, Glynwed and also Slazenger. It was a great boon to me financially and it set me up. I also have a connection with John Bell and Croyden, a huge chemist chain, and I've driven cars belonging to British Car Auctions.

Perhaps John's biggest scoop was to arrange the Nick Faldo golf shoe range manufactured by the Tecnic Shoe Company in Rushden, Northants. John possesses what the Australians would call a 'crooked leg'. He suffered from polio as a youngster and he almost died. He has to have the shoe for one leg built up which obviously makes it extremely heavy. One day he was visiting Harrods Golf Shop and Tom Bovingdon, the professional, came over and asked him if he played the game. Then he asked John to have a swing in the net and asked what his handicap was. In fact John is no mean golfer – he plays off a pretty good seven – and Tom Bovingdon became interested in whether he had trouble finding people to make his golf shoes.

Tom knew the Tecnic Shoe company and he approached them with a view to making John a pair of golf shoes. John went to Northampton to meet Ernest Newell, a director of the company, and he spoke to him about the idea of a player endorsing a range of golf shoes. The Tecnic company is a big concern, but it is a family-run affair, and so it was clear that they would have to take some time considering the prospect of designing and manufacturing a whole range of golf shoes. It took seven months to secure that contract and now we can all be happy because the shoes are sold in shops like Harrods and Simpsons and they are being exported to Europe.

17
Love and Augusta

I could hardly have wished for a better start to the 1979 European season. I was in love with a fabulous girl, who soon became my wife, and my warm-up to the 1979 campaign was a trip to America to play in the Greater Greensboro Open and the US Masters. I had spent most of the winter in the fifteenth-century Tudor cottage which I purchased with my parents and moved into during the January of 1978. So this was our first full winter tucked away in the quiet and picturesque Hertfordshire village of Ayot St Lawrence.

It was the house of my dreams because in my early days as a professional I had often passed the cottage and admired its character and considered the possibility of buying it if I ever became rich enough. My trips through Ayot St Lawrence, where George Bernard Shaw once lived, mostly took place during the winters when I helped my friend Ron Marks lay carpets. I think Ron, a really good mate to me, would have given a gambler 1000–1 against ever fitting carpets for Nick Faldo in Tudor Cottage during the early months of 1978. But that is exactly what happened. My father saw an advertisement in the local paper offering the house for sale and we had our offer of £60,000 accepted and in we moved.

From 285 Knella Road to Tudor Cottage, Ayot St Lawrence, was a long way to go in twenty years – yet it had really all happened in a period of two years when my official prize money alone totalled more than £60,000. Now, as I began to tune up for 1979, I had the perfect place, because in the garden it was possible to build a practice sand bunker and keep my swing in shape all the time. There was also room for a billiards table – great relaxation when you need to shut out thoughts of golf – and it was terrific being able to pull on a tracksuit in the mornings and go out for a run before breakfast. I got the tracksuit as a Christmas present and it wasn't too long before I had worked out several circuits around the country lanes. Keeping fit is extremely important: some rounds can take over five hours which is physically – as well as mentally – exhausting.

Melanie and I first met via the telephone. She got my number from Adrian, a friend of mine who used to go for runs with me. Mels was working for a magazine called *Jogging* and she wanted to interview a sportsman who jogged. She phoned several times, but I was on tour in Australia and New Zealand and when we finally spoke and arranged a meeting she couldn't get to the house as the road through to Ayot St Lawrence was blocked by snow. A few days later she did come over to show me what *Jogging*, a new publication, was going to look like. There wasn't time for an interview but we arranged another meeting and a photographic session.

I felt a right twerp at the photographic session because as I ran through the snow I tumbled over and came crashing down. But it went well and we arranged the interview for early in the New Year. Mels was marvellous and after she left I wished I had asked her out. I couldn't wait for the morning to come because I had decided to phone her and ask her out to dinner. The very next evening we were sitting opposite each other at the Woodside Country Club, which is near Melanie's Brookmans Park home in the Hertfordshire commuter-belt area. We were not on our own – there were four others – but the next night we went out together to see *The Great Train Robbery* in London. From that moment we were inseparable. We were out every night for the next two weeks.

Then John Simpson invited us down to stay at Broadstairs and on the way back all hell broke loose! We had a tremendous row. I wanted a particular tape on the car stereo but Mels said she wanted another and since it was her car she was going to have her way. We almost broke up – there was a whole week of indecision. We didn't see each other for a week, but after eight days I phoned and suggested we should go out to a wine bar for a chat. It was a very deep conversation and we virtually decided that we were unsuited for each other because we were two different people. But we decided to give it another whirl in order to find out for certain – and that's the best decision I've ever made. From then on we got closer and closer, but in February I had to fly out to Hong Kong for a tournament. Before I went we had a St Valentine's supper – and over the meal I proposed to Mels.

That evening we considered it best to keep the engagement secret until around May and to plan a wedding for the end of the season. But all those plans evaporated when I went out for the Hong Kong golf tournament. I enjoyed Hong Kong, although, after opening rounds of 68 and 72, I shot an 80 and missed the cut by 1 stroke. But it was a most enjoyable place and extremely fascinating. The busy people of varied nationalities are always hustling and bustling, trying to make a living, and I suppose that is the main reason why they don't suffer from strikes in the same way as we do in Britain.

Our five-star hotel had a revolving restaurant on the top and I loved the food. I think the best night was when twelve of us were taken by Charlie Chow to the Royal Hong Kong Country Club where they laid on a magnificent spread in our honour. We had a thirteen-course dinner with dishes like Peking duck and I learned how to eat with chopsticks.

I went out one day with Peter Townsend and between us we managed to barter with a shopkeeper for some silk. Peter wanted to take it home for his wife Lorna and the chap originally offered him 2½ yards for £25. But by the time we left Peter was clutching 6 yards and he had paid out just £20. I got a similarly good deal for a camera – so good that when I showed it to the Customs officer at Heathrow Airport he didn't believe me. He thought I was holding a fixed receipt and they grilled me for a long time before I was allowed to leave. It took a lot to convince them that I had really paid that price for the camera – which supported my belief that I had got a bargain!

While I was in Hong Kong, James Erskine, who ran the golf division at the International Management Group in London before he went to Australia and John Simpson took over, asked me how I was getting on with Melanie. I told him just fine and that we were thinking of getting engaged. He thought a lot of Melanie and he told me that he knew she would be right for me. It convinced me that there was absolutely no point in keeping the whole thing quiet. I came home and the first thing I told Mels was that May was out of the question for an engagement – we were going to do it now!

That led to a double problem – breaking the news to my mother and to John Simpson. John looks after my affairs with such care that I didn't know how he would take the thought of my getting married. I met him in London and we went across to his bank on the way to lunch. As we were standing there he said he was thinking of marrying his girl friend Jane. I couldn't have asked for a better 'in' and so I immediately told him my plans. He was thrilled.

It had all happened so quickly that I really felt it was going to be hard breaking the news to my mother. The point was we were really close and being an only child I could understand the far-reaching effects of Mum losing her boy. I thought I would have to work out a carefully worded speech covering all the aspects, such as how she wouldn't be losing me. But in the end I just blurted it out and Mum's face lit up. She was so pleased and I was relieved. She immediately phoned Melanie to congratulate her, which was great for both of them, and when Dad came home from work to hear the news he immediately set up a family party for the following Saturday.

We wanted to get the engagement ring for the party – we had decided to go out to the Plume and Feathers in Tewin – but after spending the entire day looking around in London we had failed to find one. All seemed lost until we called into Brent Cross on the way back and found exactly what we were looking for. So we were set for the dinner party with both Melanie's and my folks. But when we got home Mum told us that a reporter had been to Melanie's house asking about our engagement. We were stunned. Nobody was supposed to know, except for the families, but somehow the gossip writer from the *Welwyn Times* had found out and he wanted the story first. We wanted to keep it quiet. We didn't want anybody to know. So we denied it. But after chatting about it over the engagement dinner on the Saturday night, which was followed on the Sunday evening by a party at Mel's house, we decided that since it seemed to be leaking out we would be better to announce the whole thing officially.

So Monday turned out to be an exhausting day. I had to do a photographic session for the *Daily Mirror*, who wanted pictures of me in safari gear as I was soon going out for the Kenya Open. Then, at lunchtime, Mels and I were taken to Regent's Park to have pictures for the announcement of our engagement. It rated as national news because a new golf season was only a month away and I had been the top British golfer in 1978. The local papers came round to the house in the evening and so by the end of the day both of us were shattered. We hadn't settled the date, but at that time we were still planning for November . . . and it seemed a long time away.

Then I went off to Kenya for almost two weeks. I took my parents because it was about time they had a treat for all the hard work they put in during my early days. My mum had never been on a jet and I think the farthest my parents had travelled as a couple was to the south of France for a camping holiday. So it was a tremendous thrill for them and at Heathrow Airport, for the journey out, they met Henry Cooper and Dickie Henderson, who were going to play in the pro-am in Kenya and also the Jacklins, Hortons and Gallachers. It was also the first time I had been to Kenya and we enjoyed a marvellous start when we were taken on a three-day trip to the Mount Kenya Safari Club. As Britain shivered in the long-lasting winter, we sipped cold drinks under a blue sky and looked out over the stunning scenery. It can be a rough life!

We were also taken out on an escorted tour to see the wild-life and the biggest thrill was parking only a few feet away from a lion and two lionesses. The cameras came out and the animals didn't seem to be worried by our presence, but we were firmly told that if we left the van the lions would spring into action pretty quickly. So we sat tight. My golf was reasonable that week rather than outstanding and I settled for eleventh spot after rounds of 68–73–68–70. Maurice Bembridge came back to winning form when he beat Bernard Gallacher after a play-off.

But I had missed Melanie, so when I returned home we decided to bring the wedding forward to June. Once again we tried to keep it quiet, but I'm afraid that when you are in the public eye it just can't be done and fairly soon everybody knew that we planned to marry on 23 June. Before that we had a 'christening' to get through – but not the usual type. You see Mels had never seen me play competitive golf. She had watched John Simpson and me play golf at Broadstairs, but she had never seen a real live golf tournament. But she started right at the top when we travelled together to America where I was to compete in the Greater Greensboro Open before going on to make my first appearance in the US Masters at Augusta. Mels was lucky to get the time off work – she worked for her father's Sackville Design Group and we needed to twist his arm – but eventually we flew out together for the States.

We went first to the Augusta National Golf Club, scene of the US Masters, but only to take a look and for me to play a couple of practice rounds before travelling to North Carolina for the Greater Greensboro Open. I wanted to take a look at Augusta before the hullabaloo of the Masters had taken over. It was my first trip to the famous tournament, though my second to America as a professional. I had gone there in 1976 for the World Open in Pinehurst, North Carolina, but at the time I was a 'rookie' pro and I was not able to accept prize-money. I enjoyed the experience, but I missed the cut by two strokes and the six days in the States cost me £500.

Since then I have become well versed in the language of travel. It can be a mind-boggling affair – and it was much the same when Mels and I arrived in Boston on the way to Atlanta. We had been informed that there would be an hour and a half in which to change to the new flight, but by the time we arrived there were only forty-five minutes. In normal circumstances it is probably fair to say that we would not have made it. Fortunately, however, a friend in London, who works for the airlines, had passed a message through to Boston and we were given every assistance. The immigration and Customs officers worked wonders and whisked us on our way.

We arrived in Augusta at nine in the evening. The trip had taken eighteen hours and we were exhausted. John Simpson had told me that we were booked into the Augusta Hyatt, so as we came out of the airport I asked where it was. Then came the big shock – there wasn't one. I tried to recall my conversation with John and then I remembered that he had also mentioned the name 'Executive House'. So I asked if that sounded more familiar and to my relief I was told it was the local Hilton hotel. There was no doubt about it being the right place when a few minutes later a driver for the Hilton bus said he had been sent along to pick up a couple flying in from Britain.

The next morning we went out to take our first look at Augusta National. I'm glad we went there first because later, after returning from Greensboro, I realized that I had been able to discover the beauty of Augusta away from the tumultuous scenes of the tournament itself. Mels and I walked the lush fairways – although she very quickly replaced her shoes after stepping on a dead snake! Every hole at Augusta had been given the name of a different plant or shrub – from Magnolia to Azalea, Pampas to Pink Dogwood – and everything blooms virtually on the eve of the US Masters. It is a wonderful scene, with white buildings glistening in the sunshine and the rambling colonial-style clubhouse provides a truly remarkable focal point for this lovely setting. I played a couple of rounds, more as an experience than an education for the tournament, and then we flew off to the Greater Greensboro Open.

In Greensboro I played solidly, but my touch around the greens was not too hot. I realized it was a question of adjusting to the greens in America, since they are cut much shorter and it takes time to tune in to the fast pace of the putting surfaces. If I had holed a few decent putts I could have finished in the top fifteen, but as it was I had to settle for joint forty-fourth. I was not impressed with the gallery control at Greensboro, although I understand that the event that week is treated as a community holiday, but the greens were fantastic. The 18th is a long par 5, and you should finish the round by holding the green with a two-iron shot. It's impossible to play shots of that kind in Britain, which is a great pity. If we could be certain of the greens over here, we could fire two-irons into them every time and really give the spectators something to cheer.

For Melanie the Greensboro event meant an insight into what the game of golf is all about. She soon picked it up, learning the difference between a hook and a fade and the fundamentals of the game, but she had a bit of a struggle on the first day when she attempted to walk round in high-heeled boots. We went to a shoe shop that evening and bought a pair of proper walking shoes, but Melanie had still to experience the loneliness of failure which can surround us all at any time. That moment was to come at Augusta.

The curtain went up for me at the US Masters at precisely 1.26 p.m. on Thursday, 12 April. The moment had arrived for me to tee off in the first round. My partner was Billy Casper, the winner in 1970, and I approached the start with some trepidation. The crowd was huge, but I made just the opening you dream about – a birdie at the 1st. Another came at the 8th and I was beginning to think about moving into contention with a 68 or 69. Then, at the 9th, I was faced with a downhill putt of 30 feet. I knew it would be fast, but you've never seen a ball roll like this one. I struck it well and it narrowly missed the hole. It seemed to stop 5 feet past, but then it began to roll again and eventually it was no less than 40 feet away from the hole. So I completed my first 3 putt at Augusta. I dropped another at the 11th, but birdied the long 13th.

Then my world collapsed at the 14th. On my card I had it as being 140 yards to the middle of the green – an eight-iron shot for me. But my local caddie insisted it was 160 yards and that I needed a six-iron. I was confused but, considering that the caddie had been working Augusta for twelve years, and this was my first visit, I decided to split the difference and take a seven. It air-mailed the green! The ball finished 10 yards behind the back of the putting surface. What can you say? So, unhappily, I accepted a bogey 5 and dropped another at the next where the caddie had another 'black-out' and handed me a five-wood and my approach finished in water. At the end I added the score up to 73. I felt disgusted. I had played well, but I was 7 strokes off the pace.

I'm not sure what happened to my caddie at those 2 holes. He never made another mistake, demonstrating the vital part a caddie plays in advising a player. But for some reason he got it wrong twice in succession in that opening round. I did better in the second round, putting together a competent 71, and Gerald Micklem and Melanie, who walked most of the way round together, both enjoyed the day. There was not quite the same mood twenty-four hours later. I shot 79 and I found out how marginal errors can be costly at Augusta. I didn't play badly, I just hit the ball on the wrong side of the pins and kept leaving myself the difficult putts. But I was deflated. I stalked straight from the 18th to the practice ground. Poor Melanie had not experienced this situation before. She was apparently told that she shouldn't go near me – that she should let me cool down. But she went and got a cup of Coke and walked over. I looked up, winked and took the Coke. She smiled and I just whispered to her that I hoped I wouldn't play like that all year.

The last day arrived and I managed to go out in a blaze of glory with a double-birdie finish for a fighting 73. We returned to the hotel to watch on TV the final stages of the Masters and I felt for poor Ed Sneed as he cast away a 3 shot lead with only 3 holes to play, and eventually lost to Fuzzy Zoeller in a play-off. Those marginal errors, so much in evidence at Augusta, had contributed to Sneed's downfall, but once again we saw how the pressure-packed finale of a 'major' can create problems for the leaders.

Gary Player handed over the Green Jacket to Fuzzy Zoeller and we packed our bags to fly back to Britain. I had finished fortieth. It was not a great start to the season but it was the US Masters. And one day I hope to get an invitation to return to figure more prominently in this wonderful tournament.

18
Barry Willett – A Pro's Pro

There are two major stopping points for me throughout the year. One is Dyrham Park – to check my swing with Ian Connelly – and the other is at St George's Hill in Weybridge, Surrey, where another great friend of mine – Barry Willett – hangs out. Barry, however, is more than a friend – he is the only man whom I allow to check my clubs. I go to see him every four weeks – which indicates how important it is to me that the club lofts and swing-weights are kept right. Sometimes there are changes to be made because of natural wear and tear. Sometimes it is necessary to make alterations to the clubs because I'm not getting the right feel. And sometimes I just need to change a club completely.

On my return from Augusta I had the chance to go to see Barry before beginning my European campaign. I never know what will happen on a trip to St George's Hill because I've been lucky enough to hunt around his workshop and find myself a new club or two. I'm making quite a collection, but I still reckon my best find was when I spotted this shabby old driver lying on top of his bench. It had been there for three or four weeks and Barry told me later that quite a number of professionals had come in, waggled the club and put it straight back without showing a glimmer of interest. It shows how we can all think differently, because I picked it up, made a couple of practice swings and immediately questioned Barry on what he had there.

It was in a poor condition – but I had fallen in love with it. It was a 30-year-old MacGregor block and I felt certain that it was a club for me. I wanted to try it out properly so I asked Barry if he could clean the head and put in a suitable shaft. I wanted to have a go with it out on the practice range to see how it felt. I told Barry that I wanted first say and that, if after giving it a few hits I felt it was right for me, I would buy it.

Barry got to work on it and after a couple of hits I realized it was the driver for me. We agreed on a price of £50, which probably sounds quite a lot for a second-hand club, but for a prized club of that calibre a top pro wouldn't mind paying £350 or even £500. In truth you couldn't really put a price on it, because I would never part with it. It is something special to me and every time I go to see Barry it is always the first club he takes out of the bag. He still considers that it is one of the best 'sitting' drivers that he had ever had in his shop. Whichever way you put it, even when the sun is coming from different angles during a round and casting a variety of shadows, it always looks right. So it goes without saying that I used it throughout the season and it is the kind of club which I hope to carry with me for many years to come.

Picking up the driver was a bonus, but it was still important to get the whole set sorted out before starting on the European excursion. There is not much time to stop when the season is in full flow, so I wanted my clubs perfect for my attempt to improve on my 1978 third spot in the Order of Merit. My three-wood was a new Toney Penna and the five-wood was an old 1965 Toney Penna model with a key-hole insert. Penna, a former tournament player in America, is renowned as a club maker. I had got the five-wood for Augusta because of the need to hit high shots into the greens, but on the European circuit it is mostly left out of my bag because I change to a one-iron. Weather conditions are usually such that drilling a one-iron is a far safer shot than trying to hit a high-flying wooden shot into a green.

The shafts for all the wood clubs are American Dynamic 'X' – with the 'X' standing for stiffness. My shafts are very stiff and they are $\frac{1}{2}$ inch longer than average. That is to say, my driver is $43\frac{1}{2}$ inches long, the three-wood $42\frac{1}{2}$ inches and the five-wood $41\frac{1}{4}$. I have the five-wood that little shorter because I am seeking accuracy rather than length. I want to be able to chop the ball up, hook it or slice it, and the shorter shaft enables me to have more control. The irons I use are just a simple blade. I think most club designing for professionals has gone too far. I prefer to choose a simple-faced club which sits nicely and doesn't have any fancy frills like heel and toe weight. Mine are plain, solid heads and quite deep in the shank because, of course, I'm using the big ball all the time. If you have a shallow shank you get the impression that the ball is being thrown up a lot. With a big ball you need clubs that will drive the ball low.

When I go to a tournament I carry one-iron through to sand-iron and they are all equipped with Dynamic shafts. They are all stiff and $\frac{1}{2}$ inch tipped. That means the shafts are cut off $\frac{1}{2}$ inch at the head end and pushed through, which brings the first step on the shaft closer to the head and makes them a tiny bit stiffer without having to use an 'X' shaft. An 'X' shaft is thicker metal which makes it fractionally heavier. The idea is to get a club as light as possible in dead weight but to get all the weight in the head in terms of swing weight. The swing-weight machines gives you a rating – mine is $C9\frac{1}{2}$ – which basically enables you to obtain the same feel in each club. Swing weight actually relates to weight of the grip end to the weight at the head end, and once you have decided upon the best swing weight you can get a uniform feel throughout your entire set.

I use Crown cord grips. The reason is that I like to feel that the shaft is stiff the whole way through. I don't want a soft feel in my hands because at the top of the backswing, where the swing is changing from going up to coming down, there is quite a lot of leverage applied through the hands and generated on to the shaft. This is when you are trying to drive the club back down, and with a soft grip I would feel the club moving in my fingers. I like a nice solid feel. Also, for some reason, solid clubs – and I've experimented mainly with wedges and sand wedges with a hard cord grip – give you a crisper strike and it is easier to apply spin. I find with a softer grip like the Grip-rite one which most players, including Seve Ballesteros and Hale Irwin, use on tour, tend to move a little bit for me. I suppose it is due to being slightly taller, and, for those who are shorter, the softer grip may work. But when your hands are held high, you must do everything within your power to keep hold of the club and so the hard grips are very important to my game.

Spectators who get close enough to see the clubs in the bag are intrigued by the amount of lead tape I have on the clubs. Many people assume that this makes the clubs extremely heavy, but when my clubs were sent to me, the swing weight was wrong on nearly all of them and with Barry Willett I had to rebuild them again to get them right for me. I like to know – and this is extremely important – that my clubs are as simple and as solidly built as possible. I don't like any rushed or bad work done on them. It is not the thought that they might fall apart. It is simply that it breeds extra confidence to know that every one is solid. Even down to the fact that everything is in exactly the right place – like the little black fairing between the head and the shaft. They have numbers stamped on the back and if those numbers are slightly twisted, it will upset me. I'm just fussy about that kind of thing. When I take the club back I don't want to see a little white number pop out, so to speak, and distract my attention from the job of striking the golf ball.

Barry is a very methodical worker and I can trust him completely. It is vitally important to somebody like me that everything is absolutely spot on. It might not make a difference to how I play, but it does make a difference to my mental attitude. And that can be crucial.

When I change my clubs, Barry and I take them completely apart to inspect everything. In the set I picked up at the start of the 1979 tour there was some lead down in the club-head below the shaft and I had to take this out. I'm not sure whether it makes the flex of the shaft stiffer or weaker, but I do know that it makes a fractional difference that I can feel. So we got rid of all the lead, shot and glue inside the club head and refitted the clubs the way I like.

The reason I respect Barry so much is that he understands the professional's needs. He knows, for instance, that I am fussy and so everything must be absolutely right. And he makes sure that it is that way. When he refurbishes a wood, he will never touch the face. I thought he was exaggerating when he told me that if you rub the face of a wood once or twice with a piece of sandpaper it will become different. Then I had a go at altering my own three-wood. I could see a little bump where the wood had swollen, due to the wet weather and

I thought I would just rub it off. I gave it a little rub and came very close to ruining it by altering the face. I learned an important lesson : listen to the experts.

All players have clubs which are really special to them and my wedge is a 1957 Wilson harmonized model. But before the start of the 1979 season Barry's workshop turned up another new club for me – a sand wedge. It was lying there looking black and ugly. And even though I have practised thousands and thousands of bunker shots with it, I only have to leave it for a week and it goes black again. It looks as if I never use it. But the shape is perfect for me. I feel comfortable with it and that is important since I'm going to look at the club every day. It is pointless looking down at the face of a club and cringing at the way it looks back. You've got to love each other ! That means the club must look well, sit well and have a super feel. I'm learning more and more about old clubs and I'm beginning to come to terms with the fact that you shouldn't alter old clubs. For one thing, how are you ever going to get the grip back the same way? Alter it – and the feel that made the club successful for you in the first place may have gone for ever.

My interest in collecting clubs stemmed from the 1977 Open at Turnberry where a friend of mine runs a sports shop. John Moorhouse, my caddie, told me that they had Penna drivers in stock. I couldn't wait to get down there and I found one which felt great. Barry said it was the second best Penna driver he had ever seen – he rates Tom Watson's as the optimum – and it was certainly worth the £45 I paid for it. That of course, was just for the head. But I only had to play one good shot with the club and it had paid for itself. It doesn't matter if a driver costs £1000 because if it works really well for a professional it can quite easily pay for itself in a couple of weeks. Let's face it, you've only got to miss a fairway a day with a driver and that can cost you the shots that win titles.

If you have faith in a driver and every time you address it the club looks right and you hit it time and again down the middle, there cannot be any grumbles over the cost. I know, for instance, that Jack Nicklaus had a driver which a couple of years ago he had been using for eight years. The grip was wearing and drying out, but he refused to change it because he thought that if he put a new shaft in it that might make a difference to the feel and the results.

I think Jack Nicklaus's irons are standard length and I believe they have a swing weight of D1. But underneath the grips he had lead tape and he says he has done that to get a slower hand action. I can't explain why and when I picked up his clubs the first time I couldn't detect any difference. Yet in Australia, when I tried them again, I could distinguish a strange sensation and I can only put that down to the lead tape under the grips.

I suppose no two professionals are looking for the same clubs. Tom Weiskopf, for example, is about the same height as I am but he favours clubs with shorter shafts. This is because of arm length. So it doesn't follow that a guy who is short should use short shafts. Gary Player is a perfect example. He uses a longer shaft and a flatter club to get more distance. The lie on a club can be determined by the position of your hands when you grip it. So most people shorter than I will find that their hands are lower than mine when hanging loose at the side. Therefore their arc is a lot lower and flatter – they swing round themselves rather more, instead of up high, as I do. So they need a flatter lie which means knocking the toe lower down. If I tried to hit a shot like that the toe would dig into the ground.

Come to think of it, my long irons are 1 degree more upright than standard and from the five-iron onwards they are just a touch more upright. Some of the players on the tour today make a big mistake by not having their clubs with the correct lie for themselves. Mostly, I believe the clubs made in this country are too flat – in America they are slightly more upright.

The lofts on all my clubs are thoroughly checked by Barry and myself. I like the one-iron at about 16 or 17 degrees so that it is really a strong club. Then they go – two-iron (20d), three-iron (23d), four-iron (27d), five-iron (31d), six-iron (34d), seven-iron (38d), eight-iron (42d), nine-iron (46d), ten-iron (51d) and sand-wedges (56d). Keeping the lofts right is important in order that you know how far you can strike each shot with each club. I can hit my driver between 245 yards and 280 yards, the three-wood 220 to 240 and the five-wood 215 to 225. It is interesting to note that the loft on my one-iron enables me to hit the ball the same distance as the five-wood. That is why I can easily switch the clubs over and use the one best suited to the weather conditions on a particular day.

Going through the rest of the clubs, I hit the two-iron between 200 and 215 yards; the three-iron – 190–200; the four-iron – 180–190; the five-iron – 170–180; the six-iron – 160–170; the seven-iron – 150–160; the eight-iron – 140–150; the nine-iron – 125–135; and the ten-iron or wedge 90–120 yards. The sand-wedge has a maximum range of 90 yards.

Putters? They are all about feel. I began 1979 with a Ray Cook model which is made of a light alloy and very weak in the neck. For some reason, I failed to get the right look from it and I think because of that the season was to see a catalogue of putter changes. I reckon the Ray Cook got knocked slowly but surely out of shape with the continual replacing in the bag, and although I tried to work on it and get it right it just seemed impossible to get the look from the putter that I desired. I didn't hit the right putts with it and began to chop and change around with a variety of my old Acushnet Bull'seyes. I like the putter to be slightly open with a fraction of loft because in the main the greens we putt on are not consistently smooth and I want a putter which is going to get the ball rolling nicely.

Putting is so much a matter of confidence that you want to make sure at the start of the season that you immediately get on the right track. I probably made an error, although one can see this only after the event, by choosing to start my European campaign in Italy at Monticello. If I had flown straight from Augusta to the Spanish Open, where the greens at Torrequebrada are huge but fast and smooth, it might have been different. Instead, I arrived for the Italian Open and found the grass at Monticello long, the layout unexciting and the greens poor.

The first three Continental Opens of the year had resulted in wins for Brian Barnes (Portugal), Dale Hayes (South Africa) and Simon Hobday (Zimbabwe). To illustrate how important a good start is to the season, Barnes and Hayes dominated the Italian Open, with Barnsie finally winning after the play-off. For 27 holes I stayed in contention, but on the second day, when I was only 3 off the pace on the leader-board, I came home in a disastrous 41. It was windy and extremely cold and it was hard to get any inspiration on the flat Monticello course, which is close to Lake Como. I always reckon to perform better when there is some atmosphere, but nevertheless I try to plod along when things are not going well because I hate throwing away shots.

By choosing the Italian as my launching pad I undoubtedly made a big mistake. At the start of the event the course was not ready and it was only on the final day that they seemed to get it right. By then, of course, it was too late. Conditions are the same for everybody and so one shouldn't make excuses, but my point is not so much that I had a poor week but that it was a depressing send-off to the new campaign. It was important to tune-up quickly, because in a couple of weeks' time I was set to defend my Colgate PGA title at St Andrews and I was determined to retain the trophy. So, after the Italian, I only had one warm-up week remaining – the French Open.

That was a sad week for many reasons – but not really to do with my golf. The course was some way east of the city of Lyon and it was not convenient in terms of travelling. We had to hang around waiting for a 'tour' bus to come and then we faced a forty-five-minute endurance test through the crazy traffic of the town and into the country. But the sadness came on the day prior to the tournament when we got on the bus and Manuel Ramos, the young Spanish golfer who won the Portuguese Open in 1977, told us that his compatriot Salvador Balbuena had died the previous evening of a heart attack.

We were all stunned. Salvador was only 27 years old and less than twenty-four hours earlier Tony Jacklin, myself and a few other of the boys had been with him. It was a terrible shock and although I didn't know him that well I felt so sad for his family and his friends. It seemed likely that all the Spanish players would withdraw from the tournament but in the end most of them decided to compete and put the money they won to a fund for Salvador's widow.

The tournament finally began, following an anti-apartheid demonstration which was aimed at Gary Player, and ironically it was another South African, Hugh Baiocchi, who took the early lead. He was paired with Player, and Hugh reckons that the presence of his illustrious compatriot always inspires him to produce his best golf. But a 4 putt green at the 14th in the second round hit Hugh's hopes of a win and although I finished strongly with rounds of 73 and 71 it was Bernard Gallacher who won by a shot from fellow Scot Willie Milne, with Baiocchi and Seve Ballesteros another shot farther back. I finished joint fifth and so I felt much better with my form.

For big Willie Milne, who was enjoying his best-ever finish in a big European circuit event, there was still a problem. He had holed in one at the 175 yard 15th and his caddie told him that the programme stated there was a Mercedes car for the first ace of the event. It seemed that Willie, who had collected £4000 for the runners-up spot, was going to have a bonanza, but when he got back to the clubhouse the tournament organizers told him that it was a printing error and there would be no car.

Willie was far from amused – and I certainly wouldn't have wanted to break the news to this 16 stone giant. He threatened to sue and the whole affair moved into a prolonged wrangle which finally ended at the Open Championship where Willie learned he would get his car. So I suppose he got lucky – if it had been me and my luck with holes-in-one, I don't suppose I would have even ended up with a bottle of champagne!

But it was champagne that I hoped to be buying for the press again the following week when I went out to defend my Colgate PGA Championship. Having played well at St Andrews in the Open the previous year I must admit I felt confident going into the tournament. I had averaged four to five hours of practice a day to ensure that I arrived in perfect shape ready to defend. My game was nice and solid and the only aspect with which I was unhappy was the putting. I hadn't been holing out well and before I left home to drive to St Andrews I threw into the boot of the car an old centre-shafted putter which I had used to win the Hertfordshire Boys' title and the Berkshire Trophy in 1975. I hadn't used it in competition since then but for some reason my heart told me to give it a try in the first round. It worked like magic.

When I holed from 35 feet for a birdie at the 1st hole, I just knew that everything was going to go right. And when a putt of no less than 30 yards dropped at the 4th for another birdie it was clear that the putter had forgiven me for allow-ing it to gather cobwebs during the last four years. I was paired with Eamonn Darcy of Ireland and John Bland of South Africa and when I holed from 8 feet and 35 feet for more birdies at the 5th and 8th I had them scratching their heads and trying to think where they had putters hidden away! I was out in 32 and 5 footers at the 11th and 12th took me to 6 under.

Even when I drove into trouble and dropped a shot at the 567 yard 14th I wasn't worried. I could feel that this was my day and that the Old Course at St Andrews was my friend. Further putts of 20 feet at the 16th and 18th for more birdies confirmed that to be the case and I had equalled the record of 65 set by Neil Coles in the Open of 1970. It meant that Melanie and I had a picture for our home-to-be in Broadstairs, because I wanted the card framed and displayed. It was a rare round and one which left me three strokes clear of Nick Job and Gordon Brand.

Norman Mair, in the *Scotsman*, wrote, 'There is still a long way to go but yesterday was unquestionably a great performance by a 21-year-old dripping with athletic and games-playing talent.' That was a real compliment – and there didn't seem so far to go twenty-four hours later after I had compiled a round of 70 for a halfway total of 135 – 4 ahead of American Andy North.

The second round was an early start – 7.57 ! – but it worked out well because the weather got worse as the day went on. Nevertheless it was hard work because the heavy atmosphere affected the flight of the ball and all our drives were finishing about 20 yards shorter than on Day One. It meant that I was unable to carry my drive to the fairway at the 4th and that resulted in my only dropped shot on the way out. But after turning for home I birdied the 11th, 12th and 15th and everything was going to plan.

Then the dreaded Road Hole, the much-maligned 17th, once again created the inevitable problem. My five-iron out of the rough flew on me and the ball dived straight into the Road Bunker. I came out well to 7 feet but the putt was not good and I dropped another shot. I got it back with a 12 foot birdie putt at the last – that was my 14th single putt in 36 holes – and so at the end of the day I felt confident that my defence of the title was going to be successful. I had not 3 putted once and my game was sharp and solid.

One year earlier, I had been 2 strokes ahead at the halfway stage in the Colgate and accelerated away from the field to win convincingly. Now, 4 ahead, I honestly felt it was going to go the same way. I was not complacent — I knew there was a long, hard road ahead. But I had to be the favourite and so optimism was the order of the day. Then it all went wrong. Why? I just don't know. But I followed those opening rounds of 65 and 70 with 78 and 79. It was an incredible collapse, although scores soared as the weather turned icy, windy, wet and cold. But it seemed unbelievable that everything should go amiss. I was still right in the hunt after that third round of 78, but from having a 4 stroke lead I was now one behind joint leaders Gordon Brand, Des Smyth and Andy North. Looking back the 78 was the critical round, because the weather was so bad going into the final round that I reckon if I had still been 4 ahead nobody would have caught me.

I partnered Brian Barnes and Vicente Fernandez of Argentina on the last day. We all had a chance and the leading trio of Brand, Smyth and North, out last right behind us, were always looking ahead to see how we were doing. But none of us could see far enough ahead to realize that the man who was going to set the target was the incredible Gary Player. With a typical last-round charge he put together an immaculate 71 in weather which turned the last 9 holes into a nightmare for everybody on the course. It left Gary in the clubhouse with a total of 289 and then he sat back and watched us all start to collapse.

An outward 35, eight pars and a birdie 4 at the long 5th, had kept me right in there, but at the 10th I dropped a stupid shot. It put me level with playing partner Fernandez, but 1 behind Barnes, who birdied the 10th. Behind us North, like Barnes, was 4 under after making a birdie at the 10th and ahead of us Italy's Baldo Dassu did just the same to join the leaders. Gary's total was 1 over par and so he really looked out of it at the time, but suddenly a mixture of 6s, 7s and 8s went on the cards of all the front-runners and it became a real guessing game as to who was going to win.

As the weather got worse and worse, I reckoned that if I

parred my way home I would still be the PGA Champion. As it turned out I would have been right – but unfortunately I didn't get the pars. Initially, it looked good for me because Barnes dropped shots at the 11th and 13th and Fernandez did the same at the 12th and 13th. Behind, North bogeyed the 11th and 12th; Smyth bogeyed the 10th, 12th and 13th and Brand double-bogeyed the short 11th and dropped another at the 12th. In front, Dassu dropped shots at the 11th and 13th. I parred the 11th, 12th and 13th which gave me back the lead.

Then all hell let loose. Suddenly it just went. I couldn't do anything to stop the shots slipping away. We were all in trouble, but for me there was no escape. I finished 6–6–6–5–5 – dropping 7 strokes to par in 5 holes. I had come home in 44 for a 79 and it was all over. On the course the fight went on and my brave playing partner Vicente Fernandez deserved his win, if only for the fact that he parred each of the last 4 holes. That was a tremendous effort and it gave him a 75 for 288 – 1 ahead of Player and Dassu. We all collapsed – Smyth and North, for instance, both covered the back 9 in 42 – but mine was a complete disaster.

And it was a result which, unfortunately, was to set the pattern for a season in which, no matter how hard I tried, nothing seemed to go my way.

19
Open '79

The bitter disappointment of my unexpected collapse in the Colgate was reflected in the first round of the Martini International the following week. The weather had not broken and Wentworth was wet and soggy and playing every inch of its 6945 yards. This was firmly illustrated when John Morgan was the only player to break 70 on the opening day, but I left myself well and truly in trouble with a 79 which is best forgotten. It was probably a reaction round, because after the Colgate I was left looking for clues as to why my usually solid game should desert me. Losing out was not the crisis; the reason why I should fall away was the pertinent question and I desperately wanted a quick answer. The 79 hardly helped.

I was given an extra twenty-four hours to ponder the problem, because the second round was completely washed out as continual rain turned Wentworth into a quagmire. It was the first time since the 1965 Senior Service tournament at Dalmahoy, Edinburgh, that a whole day had been lost but it was a bonus for me. When the second round was eventually played I managed to get back into the swing of things with a competent 72. It was not enough to enable me to survive for the two final rounds. Australian Greg Norman went on to win and I was at least left with something on which to build.

It was fairly obvious that I needed to straighten my game right out so I missed the British Airways/Avis Open, won by Sandy Lyle on the Channel Island of Jersey, to practise and prepare for the Belgian Open at the Royal Waterloo Club near Brussels, on 7 June. Belgium, of course, had been a happy hunting ground for me and so I fancied my chance of bouncing back. A first round of 69, which left me only a stroke behind

joint pacemakers Tony Jacklin and South African Gavin
Levenson, left me in no doubt that I could make a strong
challenge for the title. And 72 in the second round kept me in
touch with a pack of challengers, who included Bobby Cole, the
South African who plays the American tour, making a rare
visit to Europe. But the second round belonged to Peter Barber,
a 22-year-old from Cambridge. He featured in yet another
hole-in-one saga, but on this occasion it brought for Peter
instant riches.

Peter's three-iron tee shot at the 195 yard 13th hole finished
in the cup and his reward was a £14,000 gleaming BMW
sports car. It was fairy-tale stuff, because he had borrowed
the 20-year-old three-iron from Eddie Birchenough, the professional at Cambridge's Gog Magog club. And at the start of
the year Peter had spent eight weeks in bed with glandular
fever. He had travelled to Belgium by train – like so many
pros on the tour Peter had to watch the pennies – but now,
after winning only £70 in four years, he was £14,000
richer.

It was a terrific day in his life, but my eyes were still firmly
glued on the £5000 first prize as the battle developed for the
championship. Everybody had expected early leader Levenson
to wilt under the pressure, but after three rounds he had an
aggregate of 207 – three ahead of Baldo Dassu. Tony Jacklin
and I were one stroke further back. Gavin, an extremely
successful amateur in South Africa, had decided the previous
November to turn professional. At 25 years of age, he was an
experienced competitor, but the heat of staying ahead in a
field of top-class professionals was expected to create problems
for him.

In the early stages of the fourth and final round that seemed
to be the case. I was still confident that I could make up the
deficit and for a long time the chance existed. Finally, however, Gavin withstood the pressure and strung together a series
of good holes to win. I finished joint second with Michael King,
who came charging through with 68, and Bobby Cole. I
suppose my closing 71 could have been much better. Gavin,
however, finished a comfortable 3 strokes ahead of us.

Now there was only one event left before Melanie and I
walked up the aisle and I was keen to provide us with a bumper

wedding present. But my opening rounds of 74, 70 and 73 were far from sufficient to put me in a challenging position for the Welsh Golf Classic over the Wenvoe Castle course. Nevertheless, I couldn't have wished for a better last round before taking a week off to get married. I blazed to a fantastic 65 to race through the field and finish tenth on 282 – only 4 strokes behind winner Mark James, who took the title following a play-off with Eddie Polland and Michael Miller. That was more like it and I drove home feeling suitably happy with the knowledge that my game was in good shape and that within a week Melanie would be my wife.

Mels and I had only got to see each other on Mondays because of the tour, which was not particularly well scheduled in 1979. It meant a lot of travelling and so I had to leave Melanie and her mother to make all the arrangements for the wedding. I just didn't have the time to devote my attention to 23 June, but finally we had got round to the eve of the big day. There were still 101 things left to do – and only eight hours in which to get it right. The most important was to pick up the ring, but I had also ordered a wedding present for Mels. It was a unique gold brooch in the shape of a golf bag, with the heads of golf clubs and even an umbrella. There was a bag tag and on one side we had our initials and on the other the date of the wedding. Mels came with me to pick up the ring and so I had to get her attention side-tracked by one of the assistants in order that I could slip the brooch into my pocket without her seeing.

I managed that successfully – but it wasn't too long before I was in the dog-house. We had been to pick up the three-tier wedding cake, but as I fumbled for the car park ticket I asked Mels to take hold of the cake. I must have let go too quickly because the bottom tier fell to the ground. Chaos! We laugh about it now, but it wasn't so funny at the time. Then Melanie's mother unfortunately reversed her car into the one belonging to Mels. And finally Mels burnt a hole in her veil. The only good thing about those disasters was that we felt we had now had the three that usually run together – and on the day everything went smoothly.

We had wanted a white Rolls-Royce as the wedding car, but because we had decided to bring the day forward we couldn't hire one. However, Ron Marks, my friend from the carpet-laying days, had a friend who owned a 1931 open-top Lagonda and he kindly agreed to come and drive it for us. It was the icing on the cake for a super day! There were 130 guests at St Mary's Church in North Mymms and the wedding reception went on until five o'clock in the morning. We ended in a motel just up the road and there was only time for a one-day honeymoon in Stratford-upon-Avon, an area Melanie knew very well from her days at the University of Warwick, where she graduated with a BA in Comparative American Studies. Then it was back to golf, and we made our way to The Belfry for the Lada English Classic.

While I had been away there had been another shock first-time winner on the tour. This time it was Rhodesian-born, but now living in South Africa, Mark McNulty. He skated home by 5 strokes in the Greater Manchester Open from Manuel Pinero of Spain. But there was to be no surprise winner of the Lada English Golf Classic as Seve stormed back to his brilliant best with a runaway triumph. The much-criticized Brabazon course at The Belfry came under fire again and Seve was the only player to finish with a sub-par aggregate. His total of 286 gave him a 6 shot win from Neil Coles and Simon Hobday. But it might have been so different if I hadn't slumped to a third round of 77.

For a while I was sure Mels and I were going to be celebrating a belated wedding present. I opened with 72 and 71 to share the lead with Graham Burroughs. Seve was a shot back in third spot. But the dream of winning the week after our wedding evaporated with that third-round disaster and a final round of 73 was sufficient only to share fourth spot with Sandy Lyle.

In retrospect, I consider that my golf in the first half of the 1979 season was really first class. I was regularly in the hunt for the titles but it just seemed that one silly round would turn the screws on me. And it happened yet again in Sweden the following week where we were playing the Scandinavian Enterprise Open over the Vasatorps course. I was in good heart and confident that my game was solid enough to produce a win in the last event before the Open championship. Once again I confirmed that to be the case when I put together a first round of 69 to share the lead with Australian Mike Ferguson. I'm not a big fan of Vasatorps course and any regard for the layout dwindled more on the second day when I crashed to a nightmare 78. Once again it had happened. From being in control and looking a leading candidate, I was back in the pack faced with the ordeal of making up 6 strokes. It proved to be too much and I closed with 74 and 71 to take joint twentieth spot as Sandy Lyle confirmed his enormous promise with his second win of the season.

There can be little doubt that Sandy's Scandinavian Open triumph will go down as one of his best-ever wins. He had opened with 73 but came through to win with rounds of 69, 65 and 69. More importantly, he had Seve as his closest challenger, but at no stage did Sandy weaken under the pressure-cooker atmosphere. Seve, of course, was right on song – he had won the English Classic the week before – and within a couple of weeks he was to be crowned Open Champion. But Sandy went head-to-head with him over those last two days and gained an outstanding win.

I returned home deflated. It had looked so good for me again, but in the end the pendulum of fate had swung against me. But there were more important things on my mind now. The Open was set to start at Royal Lytham and St Annes on 18 July. Most of my better performances had been on links courses and since I already possessed a healthy Open record it seemed probable that I would again feature well in the world's most famous golf tournament. I love Royal Lytham and the hope of breaking America's stranglehold on our championship was heightened by the knowledge that not one professional from that side of the Atlantic had triumphed on these links.

My own confidence was increased when I learned that no less a person than Arnold Palmer reckoned that I was Britain's best hope of winning. It is always nice to know that your fellow professionals have faith in you, but coming from a man as respected as Arnold this was praise indeed. I felt sure he was right, because although I had not won in the first half of the season there were signs that my game was on the brink of being very good.

The key to Lytham is often hidden in the 'loop-holes', that is to say the 8th, 9th and 10th, where a good round can be turned into a great score because of the birdie opportunities. The 8th is 394 yards long; the 9th a 162 yard par 3 and the 10th, at 334 yards, is really only a drive and a pitch. But the key is in not underrating them. If there is a strong wind, club selection can cause a few headaches. The 8th, for example, can be turned into a killer – especially if the pin is positioned in the rear left corner of the green. So I took care to check these holes thoroughly in my warm-up and by the time the curtain went up on the 108th Open I felt sure I would be able to get into the thick of things and make a name for myself.

I did – but only on the last day! I finished the Open with a 69 but my first three rounds of 74, 74 and 78 destroyed my hopes of victory. That 69 took me through to joint eighth, and I consider to finish in the top twenty in the Open is always a good performance. But the name of the game is winning, and so I was not particularly pleased with the whole affair.

Yet it was a championship that all European golfers must look back on as a tremendous success for our own circuit. For victory, of course, went to Seve Ballesteros and for once the might of the American tour had been put down. He had left stars like Jack Nicklaus, Hale Irwin, Lee Trevino, Tom Watson, Ben Crenshaw and Gary Player in his wake. It was a marvellous fillip for The European Tournament Players Division. For it has always been pointed out that to be world class one must play full-time on the American tour.

Seve, only earlier that year, had turned down that opportunity by resisting the temptation of an unprecedented offer to join the US circuit without going through the demanding task of qualifying via the 'school'. Now he had proved that a player could compete in Europe and still win a 'major'. Seve accepts, like all of us, that sooner or later it becomes necessary to play in America and show that week after week you can compete with the world's greatest players.

Ironically it was in 1979 that Seve was to lose his position as European number one. He had ruled the crest of the wave for three years, but for some reason his performances after the Open failed to give him another win. Indeed, the weeks immediately following Royal Lytham mainly turned out to be triumphs for the 'comeback man'. I missed the Dutch Open at Noordwijk, but Graham Marsh, the much-travelled

Australian, ended a long spell without a win by coming home a stroke clear of Malcolm Gregson and Antonio Garrido.

The Sun Alliance European Match-Play, which took place a week later over York's Fulford course, did produce a new winner when Des Smyth, the much-improved golfer from Ireland, stamped himself as a sound performer by overcoming, among others, Brian Barnes and Manuel Pinero on the way to defeating South African Nicky Price in the final. A display which was to mean much more to Smyth than the £6660 first prize, it helped him into the Ryder Cup team – at the expense of the next winner of the tour, Maurice Bembridge.

The Sun Alliance event had been a disaster for me. I went out in the first round – beaten by Michael Steadman. So, as the race for Ryder Cup points gathered momentum, it was clear that I was now under some pressure to remain in the running for a place in the team. When I went down to the Benson and Hedges International Open, played over the new St Mellion course in Cornwall, I was aware of the need to finish high to keep hold of my Ryder Cup spot. This time I began poorly with 75, but I worked hard all week to improve my position and after rounds of 71 and 68 I closed with an inspired 66, so at least I finished joint twelfth.

Bembridge, however, kept control from the moment he opened with two 67s and he went on to gain his first win on the European circuit since the German Open in 1975. His aggregate of 272 was 2 strokes in front of Ken Brown. For Brown it was a result which secured his own Ryder Cup place, but I was still under some pressure when the tour moved to Frankfurt for the German Open. And I still failed to make the position any clearer by finishing a lowly thirtieth as Tony Jacklin finally gained the victory which had eluded him since he won the Scandinavian Open in 1974.

If I had gone through a lean and sometimes depressing time during those couple of months, then what must it have been like for Tony Jacklin! His win in the Open in 1969, followed eleven months later by a superb victory in the US Open, had stamped Tony as a world golfing great and provided the launching pad for a golf boom in Britain and Europe. Throughout the 1979 season he had given an indication that he was ready to climb back to winning form and therefore it was really no surprise when he won the German Open by two strokes from American Lanny Wadkins and Antonio Garrido.

Nevertheless, it was a much relieved Tony Jacklin who arrived at Frankfurt airport that evening clutching the German Open trophy. His popularity amongst the players is such that in the departure lounge that evening they stood to applaud Tony when he came in – and so did the public. It was a tremendous show of emotion which reflected the sheer camaraderie which exists in the wonderful world of golf.

20

Ryder Cup Revival

I was so relieved when my Ryder Cup place was finally secure. After enjoying such a successful event on my debut in 1977 I would have been desperately disappointed if I had failed to earn a place in the team for America. I never saw making the team a problem until I struck that demoralizing spell when every week I was not finishing high enough in the fields to keep pace with my Ryder Cup challengers. It had reached a point where one needed to earn an average of £800 a tournament to stay in running – for the merit list was based on £1 a point for tournament money won and the top ten are automatically chosen. There were two places to be decided by the Ryder Cup committee of John Jacobs (captain), Neil Coles (chairman) and Seve Ballesteros (Order of Merit leader). But that would have been leaving my fate in the hands of other people. It was important to me that I should clinch the spot on my own.

For some time I was cosy in sixth spot. Then, following a couple of weeks when my earnings dropped below the £500 mark, I found myself eighth. Finally I realized that with one event remaining I was down to ninth spot and I could be over-taken by Maurice Bembridge, to name one, and suddenly Howard Clark began to come back to form. It was extremely worrying for a while and so naturally I was over the moon when the Carrolls Irish Open – the final qualifying event for points – was completed and I had my passport to America.

Maurice virtually ruled himself out of the running when he took 80 in the opening round of the Carrolls, but Clark led after three rounds and the first prize of £10,000 would have taken him above me. I had begun with a poor 78 which left me out of the battle and that put further pressure on me because Mike King, who was in tenth spot, could also jump above me. In fact Mike, who had a super year, did just that by finishing joint ninth for £1213 as I came home in joint twenty-sixth spot for £570.

Fortunately for me Clarkie's challenge faded with a last round of 75 and Mark James swooped to take the title with a sizzling 7 under par 65 over the 7097 yard Portmarnock course. He won by a stroke from American Ed Sneed, who also produced a stunning 65, and Howard slipped back to share seventh spot with Tony Jacklin. His winnings of £1650 were not nearly enough to trouble me.

Later that evening we all learned that Peter Oosterhuis, as expected, had been given one of the 'selected' spots and that the other place had gone to Des Smyth, the Match Play Champion. Des had finished twelfth in the list and so Maurice Bembridge, who was eleventh, must have felt extremely disappointed that he had been passed over. I know I would have done, but that is what makes it so important to ensure that you finish in the top ten and leave nothing to chance.

So the full team was Seve Ballesteros, Mark James, Brian Barnes, Bernard Gallacher, Sandy Lyle, Ken Brown, Antonio Garrido, Tony Jacklin, Mike King, Peter Oosterhuis, Des Smyth and myself. But before we set off for America there were two more events in which to play – the Swiss Open at Crans-sur-Sierre and the European Open at Turnberry.

I'll never understand why I went out for the Swiss event. I don't like the Crans course and, with my place secure for the Ryder Cup, it would have been better to have taken a rest. As it was, it took me no longer than a couple of days to be on the way home again. I opened with 75 and followed with a staggering 81 for a 36 hole total of 156 – 21 strokes behind halfway leader Hugh Baiocchi of South Africa. Astonishingly, Seve also missed the halfway cut and Hugh took his chance to win his second Swiss Open and the fifth Continental Open in his career by skating home by 5 shots over the Alpine course from compatriot Dale Hayes, Antonio Garrido and Italian Delio Lovato.

By the time Baoicchi was storming to victory, I was at Turnberry beginning to tune up for the European Open. I was determined that, even if I failed to make a challenge over the Scottish Links, I would at least get my game in the right shape for the Ryder Cup. In fact, it didn't go so well for me at Turnberry because I could only put together rounds of 73, 74, 70 and 75 to finish joint twenty-ninth. Victory went to Sandy Lyle, who virtually sealed the number one spot in the Order of Merit for 1979 by streaking away with a last round 65 to win the jackpot £17,500 first prize by no fewer than 7 strokes from Dale Hayes and Peter Townsend. Sandy enjoyed a stunning start with six birdies in the first 7 holes and that ruled out the prospect of a repeat of the 1978 European Open, which had ended in tremendous fashion with a play-off at Walton Heath a year earlier.

For Sandy, however, it represented a fantastic breakthrough. Just 21 years of age and the top dog on the European scene. It also illustrated that neither he nor I was wrong to make premature returns, as we both had done, from Houston University. It was a little hard to accept that the headlines now belonged to Sandy and not, as they had done only twelve months earlier, to Nick Faldo, but nevertheless I felt that my game was coming back at Turnberry and so I joined the Ryder Cup team at Heathrow Airport the next day looking forward to the week ahead.

We flew to Washington, where we were met by Billy Casper, the American captain, and from there we took a one hour flight to Lewisburg airport. We travelled as a party of sixty, together with wives, team officials and the press, and Melanie and I were thrilled with the next part of the journey. There were a huge number of black limousines to take us all to White Sulphur Springs, a small town in the heart of West Virginia, and once there we arrived outside the entrance to the Greenbrier Hotel.

The programme notes stated that the Greenbrier is a resort just two years younger than the United States but as contemporary as your morning newspapers. It is said that in 1778 a certain Mrs Amanda Anderson, long helpless with rheumatism, was brought, slung on a litter between two horses, to the edge of the mineral-loaded, brimstone-smelling waters of White Sulphur Springs. Then she was placed in a hollowed tree trunk and immersed slowly into the sulphur water. Hot stones were dropped in to help promote the powers of the water. Mrs Anderson apparently leapt out of the water and screamed, 'I'm cured! I'm cured!'

True or not, the incident attracted more and more people to the area and White Sulphur Springs became renowned as one of the country's leading resorts, with the dining-room of the Old White, originally called the Grand Hotel, seating 1200 guests at one time. Guest accommodation totalled 700 in the hotel and 1300 in the so-called Old White Cottages.

It was not until 1914 that the first 18 hole golf course was opened, known as the Old White Course, but the growth of the game and the popularity of the area led to another 18 holer – The Greenbrier – being opened only ten years later. Following an inspection the great Walter Hagen was quoted as declaring it to be the most interesting resort layout he had ever seen. In 1936 Sam Snead, then only 23 years old, took on the position as professional at the Greenbrier and since then the resort has become more and more golf orientated – Henry Cotton won a spectacular reopening tournament in 1948 – and the high spot of its golfing history was now ready to unfold with the 23rd Ryder Cup match. I was proud to be part of it.

I was immediately impressed with the hotel, but it was the practice facilities which made me feel like a kid again. Throughout the year in Europe the driving ranges seemed to have got smaller and worse but now here was a fantastic practice ground. The turf was super and you could stand there and just hit ball after ball. Too often in Britain it takes ages to hunt around for a piece of decent ground which isn't full of weeds. And let's face it, our climate means that on most occasions you stand there in the mud and the rain trying to put your swing right.

At the Greenbrier it was so different, with thousands of new balls to hit and well-placed targets at which to aim. Every day I spent at least two hours in practice and I thoroughly enjoyed hitting 300 balls off one after another. 'Oosty' came over and asked me if I normally hit that many. But I just told him that I felt so good and I wanted to practise as much as possible to get my game in top shape. I knew it would come right and sure enough everything began to fall into place. There was a need to start striking the ball a little higher and I worked hard to get the right swing. Talking to Ian Connelly after I came home from America we realized that in Britain, with the wind and the rain, I had begun to stoop, but in the sunshine of West Virginia I stood up more and struck the shots in the correct manner. The irons began to feel so good and after spending a couple of hours in the bunkers I felt my short game coming right back. It was a transformation and I began to realize how Amanda Anderson must have felt when she stepped out of the waters and walked away!

At that point, I began to believe that we had a great chance of winning the Ryder Cup. No British team has ever won on American soil, but I suppose it is fair to say that we were starting a new era. For the first time Continental players were in our team, which meant we were now a European outfit and so we hoped to celebrate the joining of forces with a surprise win. I think my own form as an individual encouraged me to think that the week ahead might be successful and I felt confident.

Before we stepped out for that first day's play there was a worry that the Ryder Cup might be blown off the map as Hurricane Frederick threatened to sweep north from Florida and create a 'rain-out'. Contingency plans had to be made with the threat of continuous rain and a downfall of 10 inches predicted in forty-eight hours. The Americans could well have been in trouble because Hubert Green's house on the south coast, only 200 yards from the sea, was at one time threatened by the hurricane. The possibility of Hubert's departure south lingered as American skipper Casper heard the news over breakfast twenty-four hours before the start of the match that Tom Watson was out of their team.

Watson had always insisted that his appearance depended entirely upon the time of the birth of his first child. So when he heard during the night that his wife Linda had gone into labour it was action stations and a flight back home to Kansas City. Casper, with eleven children of his own, understood the situation, and Mark Hayes, who shot a record 63 in the 1977 Open at Turnberry, was telephoned and told to make his way to the Greenbrier. The loss of Watson was bad news for the Americans and it clearly disrupted their plans, but Casper was relieved to learn that Hubert's wife Karen had evacuated the family home and, although there was no news of the extent of the hurricane damage, he had no plans to leave.

So we were all as ready as we would be and I had learned from captain John Jacobs that the 'old firm' of Oosterhuis and Faldo would be returning to action. Oosty had endured a long hard struggle in America and throughout 1979 he had struggled more than ever. But he arrived at the Greenbrier bolstered by a couple of fine results – four sub-70 rounds in the Greater Hartford Open for joint tenth place and a blazing final round of 63 to finish fourth in the Westchester Classic. That was good form and John Jacobs, who was quick to take a look at Oosty's swing, didn't take long to agree that he was looking sharp and ready for the job. We were both ready.

The gun went up on the 23rd Ryder Cup – and Oosty and I made a blazing start. We had been paired to meet Andy Bean and Lee Elder in the morning foursomes and we collected four birdies in a row from the 2nd. Yet we were only one up and looking back I still find it hard to believe. I had made a birdie at the par 4 2nd to put us 1 up and we halved the long 3rd in birdie 4s. Elder holed from 35 feet for a 2 at the short 4th; I followed him in from 25 feet for the half. I wedged to 2 feet for an easy birdie at the long 5th but Bean squeezed a half by holing from 18 feet. Then, would you believe it, Elder rapped home a 20 foot putt at the 6th to square the match. It was great stuff. Thankfully the hurricane had swung away, but a downpour brought a forty-minute break and I must admit it seemed to change the direction of those opening foursomes. We had all begun well but now the Americans were firing back.

Ballesteros and Garrido, from 2 up after 2 holes, suddenly found Larry Nelson and Lanny Wadkins a tough pair to handle and the Americans began to take the initiative. Brown and James looked set to hand out a shock defeat to Lee Trevino and Fuzzy Zoeller, but after being 1 up after 6 they began to fall behind. In the other match, the solid Scottish pair of Barnes and Gallacher were struggling – 3 down after 6 to Hale Irwin and John Mahaffey.

I was confident that Oosty and I could still win, but Bean and Elder were irresistible. They had eight birdies in 11 holes

from the 3rd, and although I managed to get up and down
from bunkers at the 7th and 9th for valuable halves we eventually lost 2 and 1. Barnes and Gallacher spared us all a few
blushes and saved a first morning whitewash with a superb
recovery to beat Irwin and Mahaffey 2 and 1.

Of the four European pairs Oosty and I had the best figures
– 6 under par for the 17 holes – and with those figures we
would have won any of the other three matches. So we were
not too disappointed until learning that skipper John Jacobs
had dropped us for the afternoon foursomes. The affair was
quite confusing. First of all, John came out to us at about the
12th and informed us that we would be playing in the afternoon. It is nice to learn early on so that you can start preparing
yourself for another match – in other words you don't allow
yourself to calm down and relax. You want to remain razor
sharp and competitive. So we said fine, and then he told us
to go and make some birdies and so we did just that – even
though they were not enough to beat Bean and Elder. Then,
when we had finished, he said, 'Right, you're now dropped.'

It didn't mean a lot to us at the time, but I bet Oosty was
wondering what was going on, since he was almost acting as
vice-captain. He was the man on the team with a deep knowledge of the Americans and since we had both played outstanding golf in the morning it seemed only fair to give us
another crack. But we were dropped. It was a great pity
because the following day in the foursomes we proved, even
though Oosty was struggling a little with his game, that we
were operating perfectly as a partnership. We finished 3 under
par for the 13 holes that it took us to thrash Bean and Tom
Kite 6 and 5. We didn't have a single bogey and we absolutely
demolished the opposition.

It was the kind of sparkling win the side needed because in
the foursomes on the afternoon of the first day we had lost
$2\frac{1}{2}$–$1\frac{1}{2}$ to leave us trailing $5\frac{1}{2}$–$2\frac{1}{2}$ and with something to do
to make it a match. But in those second-day foursomes Jacklin
and Lyle teamed up to win and Barnes and Gallacher won
again and so we came into lunch only $6\frac{1}{2}$–$5\frac{1}{2}$ down and with
everything to play for. It was beginning to look as if we could
make a go of it. But in the afternoon fourballs, the last team
section before the final-day singles, Oosty and I were the only

winners – finishing 5 under par for a 1 hole victory over Elder and 'substitute' Mark Hayes.

That match had a tremendous finish because Hayes holed a fantastic putt right across the 17th green for a winning birdie 2. It was down the slope and it was going so fast but the ball horseshoed round the cup before dropping. That cut our lead to 1 with 1 to play and we knew the pressure would be on just to halve the last hole and win the match. I hit a really good drive but too far and it got caught on a rough edge on the right-hand side of this 550 yard hole. I then hit a five-iron up the fairway and Oosty, playing very solidly, was 60 yards short of the green in 2. I was undecided about what club to hit and eventually took an eight and the ball got knocked down by the wind and fell into a bunker on the right-hand side. Then Oosty played a poor pitch and left the ball at the bottom of the upward sloping green.

It suddenly looked as if I was the one who was going to have to make the 5 if the hole was to be halved and the match won. But I hit a poor bunker shot – leaving the ball 8 feet short. Both Hayes and Elder got close enough to be given certain fives and Oosty went next and struck his putt 6 feet past. I was mad because it now looked as if we might not win and having played the best golf I didn't want that to happen. So I stood over the ball for my putt and told myself that I just had to make it to ensure that victory was ours. It went straight in. Oosty and I had won our last two matches, making four wins out of five in two Ryder Cups.

Looking back, I think it is fair to say that John Jacobs should have played us on the afternoon of the second day. I don't go along with the theory of needing a rest. If you are playing well then you just don't get tired and I was loving every minute of my golf in America.

I wasn't so pleased when I found myself 3 down after only 4 holes in the singles against Lee Elder. For one thing it hurt my pride and for another we knew that there was an outside chance of success and I desperately wanted to do my bit for the team. I had messed up the 1st, wedging into a bunker, and I was unlucky at the 2nd where my approach jumped through the green. Then Elder made a 2 at the 4th when he holed a 12 foot putt.

But then I really turned things round. I was a bit mad because I had hit only one bad shot and Elder was 3 up. But my wood approach to the green at the 546 yard 5th was a real beauty. I had to jump on it to give it a chance and even in the air it didn't seem as if the ball would make it. But it finished 20 feet from the hole for a 2 putt winning birdie 4. That gave me a real boost and I launched into some real attacking golf. I turned 2 down, but won the 11th with a birdie 3 and Elder took 4 at the short 11th and we were all level. Then I won the 12th with a birdie and the 14th with a par to go 2 up.

Now I was in complete command, but I had a hell of a decision to make at the 412 yard 16th where the second shot is over water to a two-tier green. I was 2 up with 3 to play and Elder was on the green and not too badly placed. With the pin on the bottom tier, I didn't want to under-club so that the ball fell into the water. I took out the eight-iron and gave the ball a kind of chop so that it would float in with enough carry, but soft enough to stop quickly and give me a decent putt. It finished 18 feet from the hole and I saw my chance. I was determined not to waste it and give Elder the chance of coming back. My putting was much better throughout the week, because of the fast, and true greens, and I gave it every chance and in it went.

All in all it had been a great week. After a disappointing year I had redeemed myself and at least done my bit for my country and my team. There is nothing like the Ryder Cup. It is such a great feeling to play for your country. The Americans gave me a few pats on the back, and it was nice to feel that I had shown, even though it was late in the year, that my game had not gone forever.

Sadly, of course, we didn't win the Ryder Cup. The final day had begun controversially when Billy Casper had asked for the return of the envelope in which he had sealed the name of the player he could withdraw in the singles, in the event of one of our players being injured or ill and unable to play. As it happened, Mark James was out – he had played only the first morning fourballs with Ken Brown, and they had lost 3 and 2 to Trevino and Zoeller, with James feeling a shoulder strain.

There followed an unfortunate affair, when Ken Brown

apparently did not co-operate in the afternoon foursomes with
his new partner Des Smyth, and they crashed 7 and 6 to Irwin
and Kite. Now Casper asked for the envelope back, presumably
wanting to change the name of the man he would leave out in
the singles to compensate for James's absence. Sportingly, our
captain John Jacobs agreed, making no fuss, and when the
envelope was returned and opened, it was Gil Morgan who
was left out.

Apparently, Trevino's name had been inside the first
envelope, but the change meant that Sandy Lyle was now due
to play the formidable Super Mex, instead of Morgan in the
last singles match. That favoured the Americans, because Lyle
had been drawn to play Morgan in one of the first matches,
and we all felt that Lyle could have given our team an early
boost by beating Morgan and a win like that might have given
our effort more impetus.

But, in the end, we had played our best and lost. We were up
against their finest players and we did the best we could. But
on that final day Gallacher, Brown and I were the only singles
winners, and the team went down 17–11. The big disappointment was that Ballesteros and Garrido, so strong in practice,
never struck winning form. In contrast, Gallacher, who beat
the effervescent Lanny Wadkins in the singles, had a super
week and so did I.

For Brown, there was some consolation in a slender 1 hole
win over Zoeller, but both he and James came under fire from
officials and the press for their conduct on and off the course.
The result was that, some time after the team's return home,
Brown was banned from international team golf for a year and
James was fined £500, and both had their Ryder Cup match
fees of £1000 withheld. I was not a member of the disciplinary
committee, so it is not for me to comment on the actions of
the two players in America, but I've known Ken since our
Hertfordshire Colts days and as I have said before he has
always gone his own way.

Poor Ken was back in hot water the following week when
he was sent out early in the morning in the SOS Talisman
Tournament Players Championship because of his reputation
for being a slow player. The event was at Moor Park and after
my return to form in the Ryder Cup I felt that it would be

possible for me to gain a much-needed win. Knowing Moor Park really well, I like the course, but on this occasion the greens were not as good as usual, and after opening with a couple of solid 72s I carded a third-round 78 and eventually finished twenty-third. Mike King – who, ironically had been given only one chance to play in the Ryder Cup clash – gained one of the most popular wins of the season by edging home by a stroke from that superb club professional Brian Waites.

That left only one remaining chance on the European circuit for me to gain a victory in 1979 – the Dunlop Masters over the new and picturesque Woburn course. Again it was not to be. I opened with a competent 71, a couple of shots off the pace, but then 76 and 75 pushed me right back into the pack and out of contention. In the end I finished joint 19th and it was Australian Graham Marsh, one of the most popular golfers in the world, who scored a £10,000 win – pipping the ever-green Neil Coles and Japanese Isao Aoki by a shot.

So 1979 in Europe was over. The high spot was the Ryder Cup. I think the low spot came after the Dunlop Masters when it was all over. I went back to our flat at Broadstairs and I felt upset because it was the end. There was nothing I could do about it. All year I had stayed hopeful that there would be another win. But now I felt flat and very disappointed. The only other times I felt really low were the weeks when I practised very hard, played very well and didn't get any reward. It seemed to happen to me in 1979 more than ever before in golf and I suppose if you are going to have a year in your career like that then it is best to have it behind you. At times I had wondered what I needed to do to get it going, but it seemed that whatever I tried things would go against me.

At the end of the season I went to see Ian Connelly to try to evaluate the reasons behind my lack of success throughout 1979. I started the year feeling terrific after a hard winter of work and I struck the ball solidly and authoritatively throughout the summer. I never had a spell when I couldn't hit it. So I was in a dilemma as to know why it hadn't gone so well.

I think it stemmed from putting very poorly and if you lose your confidence in that particular area it will spread very rapidly through the rest of the game. If you miss a green you place extra pressure on yourself because you know that you've got to chip the ball close. I was missing 4 footers and so I needed to get the ball dead to feel certain that I wasn't going to drop a shot. That, of course, put a burden on my chip shots. Then it goes back to standing in the middle of the fairway and saying to yourself that if the approach misses the green you are almost certainly going to drop a shot because you are not chipping or putting as sharply as you might be.

Then, if I started playing really well and knocking the ball into 10 or 5 feet from the pin, I would miss the birdie putts and there is nothing more infuriating than throwing shots away like that. I would get very annoyed because instead of being 4 under par, which is what I should have been on several occasions, I began to shoot 74s and 75s and 76s. I had played well for those scores, but missed the chances.

I said to Ian that I had got fed up with saying that the ball wasn't running for me. I didn't want to sound a bore on the subject, but you do need a little slice of good fortune to win at this game. When luck is with you it always seems, for instance, that if you hit the ball into a small copse of four or five trees you will walk in there and find you have a swing. Then, when luck goes against you, you find that the trees are stopping your backswing or blocking the route to the green. These are not excuses – and I know you make your own luck – but it was good to know that Ian agreed with me.

It had been one of those years when even a machine like Liverpool Football Team would have not stood a chance of winning the First Division title if they had experienced the same kind of misfortunes as I did. Luck is part of the game – and you need it in any walk of life. Ian had watched me play at Moor Park and he came up to me after that and he admitted that the gremlins appeared to be out to get me.

When I look back it seems that I might have tried to play the holes too well. To some people that might sound stupid, but on many courses you simply do not get rewarded all the time by playing good golf. If the pin, for example, is in a tough position I happen to be the sort of guy who wants to go at it. To me it is a challenge to get the ball as close to the hole as possible wherever the pin is placed. If it comes off you don't necessarily rave about that one shot but I set my own standards by successfully executing such shots. But it has to be said that the guy who chooses the conservative route, which might mean playing 20 yards left of the pin to avoid hitting over a sand or water hazard, will probably make a solid score time and time again.

I want the chance to make a birdie putt because essentially I am a winner. That is not bragging; it is a meaningful statement. There are countless players on the tour who will regularly finish in the pack and collect what amounts to their expenses for the week. Those are the conservative golfers. But I believe winning stems from playing the bold shots, setting up the birdie putts and having the confidence to rap the ball into the cup. My year boiled down to the fact that I went for the big shots, they didn't come off and my putter never got lukewarm.

21

Defying the Odds

When I started out in golf I found it lonely and frustrating. Then came success. Now, with a run of failures, a new pressure had built up. I try not to allow it to affect my mental state because basically I want to enjoy life. So I make sure I have a fresh mind every week. But it's noticeable the difference that winning and losing makes. It is not merely reflected in your bank balance; it is mirrored in your personal life. When you are playing well everyone wants to talk to you. Struggle? And you find out who your real friends are.

It is at times like these that you find it harder to be away from home. I left at the end of the European tour to play a couple of tournaments in Japan, but after narrowly missing the cut in the first event I found myself wanting to come home to see Melanie. So I withdrew from the next tournament and flew back to Britain. It was a decision with which not everybody agreed. Yet I'm sure it was the right one.

I didn't make that decision lightly. It was based on the knowledge that in previous years I had gone away for winter tours which had proved complete disasters. I didn't want to make the same mistake and burden myself with more pressure, so I came home in order that I could have a week to prepare properly for a tour to South Africa. Melanie was coming with me and so that was great. But I knew, after my indifferent season in Europe, it was important that when I flew out to South Africa I felt in the right frame of mind to compete on the 'Sunshine Circuit'.

I was extremely hopeful about South Africa for sentimental reasons. In the winter of 1976–7, my first as a professional, I went out there and I returned to enjoy, in 1977, the season which really launched my career. In the two winters since then

I had tried two other tours – and both had been flops from a personal point of view.

In 1977–8 I embarked on a mini world tour – taking in Morocco, South America and then Manila, for the World Cup in which I was representing England. At the same time I was trying to overcome the after-effects of glandular fever and I simply placed too much strain on my energy reserves. I thought at the time that I had been foolish. It was crystal clear that I should have gone to South Africa and that is exactly what I planned to do in 1978–9. Yet once again my arrangements were completely messed up.

The trouble was that I had enjoyed such a super season in Europe in 1978 that my management agency were able to negotiate a good contract for me to play on the Australian and New Zealand tours. It seemed a sensible idea to play where the top money was on offer, but for two major reasons it all went wrong.

First I was exhausted from that long, hard and demanding year. Then I went out there with a new set of clubs which turned out to be a complete disaster. They had felt good in practice but in competition they fell well short of what I expected and required. The shafts were a fraction too short and too stiff and although I tried to work on them myself while I was in Australia I just couldn't get them right. The ball would rise too quickly off the blade in the wind and I was losing distance. So my game suffered.

I also got a very cold reception in Australia. To this day I cannot understand why it happened. I never expected the band to be playing when I stepped off the plane. But for some reason I found the guys who come over and play on our tour in Europe were different people. One would have expected them to be happy and hospitable on their home ground. Instead they took the stance that Nick Faldo was on their soil and because he had done well in Europe that season it didn't mean a damn in Australia. It was my first experience of 'pommy-bashing'.

My back was up from the moment I arrived for the Australian PGA tournament because they told me that my entry was wrong. Wrong? I hadn't even done the entry – that is organized by the office and since they do millions of them it is hardly likely that they would make an error. Of course,

I played in the event and I still wonder if the whole episode was sparked to put early pressure on me.

My two lasting memories of Australia are of meeting the England cricket team, touring there at the time, and watching them play in both Melbourne and Sydney – in fact, Ian Botham and Geoff Miller also came to watch me in action – and of one Australian golfer – David Good. He tried to make me feel at home, but generally, on their home circuit, the Aussies didn't want to know me. So it was good to move on to New Zealand, a lovely country where everybody was friendly, but by the time I got there it was clear that the hectic season, coupled with the pressures of Australia, had combined with the poor set of clubs to ruin my game. I missed the 54 hole cut in the New Zealand Open and flew home by Air New Zealand.

So now, as another British winter approached, I was determined that this time I would do it right. A good majority of my best friends on the circuit are South Africans – chaps like Dale Hayes, Hugh Baiocchi and John Bland. So it was like going to meet a few mates, except this time I would be playing on their circuit. A lot of work had gone into building the 1979 'Sunshine Circuit' into a world-class affair and a number of American players were competing. So the competition was going to be tough. Unfortunately the original prize-money targets were not reached and South Africa probably has some way to go before it finally sets up a tour which is right there at the top. But nevertheless it is a lovely country, the courses are splendid and for me going there was the right decision to make.

For, after all the anguish and apprehension of 1979 in Europe, it took me only one tournament in South Africa to be back in the winners' enclosure. I won the ICL International at Kensington, on the outskirts of Johannesburg, and I cannot relate what that win meant for me. I'm not sure how I would have approached 1980 if I had gone through 1979 without gaining a single success.

Melanie and I arrived in Johannesburg ten days before the start of the ICL event. So I took the chance to have a close study of the Kensington course – and I liked what I saw. But it was clear, and the record books emphasized the point, that it would need low scoring to take the title. In 1978 no fewer than twenty-four players closed with sub-par aggregates and there was a galaxy of low rounds. So I knew that I would have to get away fast if I was to have the chance of becoming only the second 'foreigner' to capture the ICL crown following Peter Townsend's win in 1976.

In fact, the early fireworks came from one of the younger South Africans – Dennis Watson. He added a super second round 65 to an opening 67 for a stunning halfway score of 132, which was evidence enough that low scoring was again going to dominate the tournament. But I had made my best start since the Colgate back in May. A 68 and 66 put me only 2 strokes off the pace and my heart began to beat to the prospect of immediate glory in South Africa.

I knew the third round would be important. Throughout the season in Europe I had regularly come a cropper on the third day. Once again I didn't play well, but this time I managed it much better and instead of a disaster I managed to come in with 69. It wasn't great, because it left me 6 strokes behind pacesetter Watson, but I still felt that I was in with a chance.

Even though I was in a foreign country, I had the luxury of a lot of people rooting for me on that final day. Glynwed, the company to which I have an attachment in Britain, had suggested to an associate company – Defy Industries Ltd in South Africa – that they look after me while I was in their country. They were super to me and clearly hoped that I could land a victory in the first event in which I competed. And George Blumberg, the Johannesburg industrialist and one of golf's biggest friends, was also cheering me on.

I went out with the thought that I would have to blaze something like 63 to topple Watson and company. So I had to make a great start – and I got a flier. It is extremely important to grab a couple of early birdies if you are to have a good score at Kensington. And after 6 holes I was 3 under par and Watson and John Fourie and Nicky Price – all showing signs of nerves as the pressure built up – knew they had a tiger on their tails. I was now 4 off the pace and the tension was mounting.

A birdie at the 8th kept my attack flowing nicely, while all round me the challengers for the title were struggling. Poor Watson, after playing so well for so long, dropped 5 shots between the 9th and 13th. Nicky Price ran up an 8 at the par

5 8th and John Fourie let 3 shots go to par between the 6th and 10th. I knew that my chance had come, but at the 13th I had to get up and down from 40 yards to save my par and remain in the picture.

Then, when I missed the green at the short 15th, I thought it might be all over. At the time my calculations put me 3 behind and I felt certain I was going to need a grandstand finish to claim the title. But as I got near to the green I permitted myself a look at the leader-board – I was ahead! It was unbelievable. From 6 behind I was now leading with 4 holes to play, but I still had to save my par at the 15th. I chipped the ball to 1 inch and holed for the 3. My mind was working overtime. When I'm in with a chance of winning my brain works so fast because I'm trying to work out what my rivals can do – and what I need to do to ensure success. So when I missed a short putt for a birdie at the 16th I was well aware that it could all slip away.

I drove well at the 343 yard 17th, but the ball finished in an old divot mark. Now all the frustrations of my 1979 year in Europe came racing back. Surely Lady Luck was not going to twist against me once more. I cleared my head, took out the wedge and struck the shot to 6 feet from the hole. Allan Henning, the experienced South African golfer, had already set the target in the clubhouse with a 13 under par total. I was 14 under par now and I knew if I could hole this putt it would mean John Fourie, my only serious rival still left on the course, would need to finish with two eagles. I lined up the putt, gave it a good stroke and in it went.

15 under par, 1 hole to play and the ICL International was at my mercy.

The last hole at Lexington is 411 yards long. It is a fairly straightforward hole, although a bunker on the right can present problems, and I kept nice and calm for the drive. It was a good one and I was left with a six-iron to the green. If I could get it close enough then a birdie would surely put the issue beyond all doubt. It would give me a 16 under par total of 268. It would also give me a record-equalling 65. And it would give me another title at long last.

I put everything I had left into that six-iron – and it finished 14 feet from the hole. Now for the putt and the title. It never looked like missing and the ball dived into the cup. I fisted the air. Two youngsters raced on to the green to try to retrieve the ball. 'Uncle' George Blumberg wept with delight, Mels grinned. The record crowd cheered. The sun shone.

And Nick Faldo was champion!